TRIATHLON
SWIMMING

TRIATHLON SWIMMING

MASTER OPEN-WATER SWIMMING

with the Tower 26 Method

Gerry Rodrigues
with Emma-Kate Lidbury

Boulder, Colorado

Tower 26® is a registered trademark of Aquatic Management Services.
TAP® is a registered trademark of Aquatic Management Services.
Ironman® is a registered trademark of World Triathlon Corporation.

4745 Walnut Street, Unit A
Boulder, CO 80301–2587 USA

VeloPress is the leading publisher of books on endurance sports and is a division of Pocket Outdoor Media. Focused on cycling, triathlon, running, swimming, and nutrition/diet, VeloPress books help athletes achieve their goals of going faster and farther. Preview books and contact us at velopress.com.

Distributed by Ingram Publisher Services

Library of Congress Cataloging-in-Publication Data

Names: Rodrigues, Gerry, author. | Lidbury, Emma-Kate, author.
Title: Triathlon swimming: master open-water swimming with the Tower 26
  method / Gerry Rodrigues with Emma-Kate Lidbury.
Description: Boulder, Colorado: VeloPress, [2020] |
Identifiers: LCCN 2020001763 (print) | LCCN 2020001764 (ebook) | ISBN
  9781948007054 (paperback) | ISBN 9781948006187 (ebook)
Subjects: LCSH: Swimming—Training. | Triathlon—Training.
Classification: LCC GV837.R633 2020 (print) | LCC GV837 (ebook) | DDC
  797.2/1—dc23
LC record available at https://lccn.loc.gov/2020001763
LC ebook record available at https://lccn.loc.gov/2020001764

This paper meets the requirements of ANSI/NISO Z39.48-1992 (Permanence of Paper).

Cover design by Kevin Roberson
Interior design by Vicki Hopewell
Photography by Gani Piñero, except for front cover and p. 181 by Shigemitsu Ichinomiya,
  and p. 168 courtesy of swim2000.com (except for neoprene shorts, courtesy of Roka)
Illustrations by Neal McCullough

20 21 22 / 10 9 8 7 6 5 4 3 2 1

This book is dedicated to the thousands of athletes I've coached throughout my career. Collectively, those experiences allowed me to share this knowledge.

CONTENTS

PREFACE

I believe many of us are born to be or do something in particular. The trick, of course, is finding your passion and giving yourself to it fully, without reservation. Sadly, many people don't, often dismissing it as quixotic. I'm one of the lucky ones; I found my passion early in life.

With humble means but a fortunate upbringing, I grew up on the Caribbean island of Trinidad. I began swimming at the age of 7. Apparently, I had pestered my parents, Georgie and Diane, for the three years prior, so they finally gave in and took me to the local YMCA to sign up for the swim team.

From that point on there was no stopping me. My passion for swimming and the life it gave me continued to blossom. I never missed a workout; I ate up the training dished out and begged for more. By the age of 10, I had set lofty goals for myself. It was 1972, the year of the Munich Olympics and Mark Spitz's incredible seven gold-medal performances. I remember the 1972 Games with near-perfect clarity: I would secretly set my alarm for 3 a.m. so I could listen to the swimming competition on the radio. As the sportscaster described each gold medal Spitz won in world-record time, I imagined the day when I would strike Olympic gold and proudly stand on the podium as my island nation's anthem played for all the world to hear.

Despite numerous fairy tales to the contrary, wishing doesn't always make things so. I never fulfilled the Olympic dream I shared with millions of other kids. I never won an Olympic medal of any sort. In fact, I never even made the Olympic team. Yet who could have predicted that 20 years later that same skinny, ambitious kid from a tiny third-world country would end up coaching Spitz at the University of California–Los Angeles (UCLA)?

That memorable year also marked the start of my open-water training. Our swim coach, Mr. Peter Samuel Senior, was preparing us for the island's annual 4,000-meter open-water race with three months of 6 a.m. sessions, three or four days a week. Swimming in the ocean only further ignited my passion for swimming, and I knew for certain I'd be a lifelong swimmer. I felt more at ease in open water, totally free. One of my oldest friendships was forged over the hundreds of miles of swimming in preparation for Trinidad's annual open-water race. Richard Hoford and I had swum together from the age of 8, and, as like-minded boys with similar speed and talent, we pushed each other to become better. Over the years, I won that race multiple times, along with another 100 open-water victories. Looking back, I can see that Mr. Samuel was providing my teammates and me nothing short of visionary coaching. We were immersed in advanced open-water skills and strategy at a time when few athletes or coaches were taking to the ocean to train. These skills laid the foundation for my career, and Mr. Samuel had a tremendous impact on me.

By the time I was 12, our community staged a two-hour swimathon to raise money for the construction of a new pool. Tasked with swimming as far as I could over two hours' time, I dutifully began. When I hit two hours, I looked up to the pool deck only to find everyone screaming at me to keep going. My 1:15-per-100-meter pace had me within reach of 10,000 meters. I hit that prestigious mark in 2:05. My engine, my drive, and my passion were there right from the start; I was an insatiable swimmer.

My parents played a huge role in my development, on both the practical and emotional levels. My mom enabled everything to happen, running our family home with seamless ease; I could not have asked for a better, more supportive mother. My father, despite working 80-hour weeks, always made the time to take my teammates and me to swim practice, driving around the neighborhood to pick up as many as 13 of us, which was perfectly acceptable at the time. He taught me the importance of always showing up on time, working hard, giving your best, and honoring your commitment and your coach. The echo of his words has filled my head thousands of times at races big and small: "The guy next to you is hurting just as much as you; otherwise he'd be ahead."

My early years of swimming rewarded me with an athletic scholarship to Pepperdine University after a stint at Saddleback Community College in Mission Viejo, California, where I trained under the incredible guidance of legendary coach Flip Darr. I learned a great deal from him about the mechanics of workouts, set construction, and swimming at different speeds and intensities—knowledge that I continue to use in my program today.

Throughout my collegiate career and beyond, I competed on numerous Trinidad national teams, travelled to scores of countries, amassed national and world titles and records as a masters swimmer, made a 28.5-mile swim around Manhattan Island, and made many friends throughout the world.

In the early 1980s, while finishing college at Pepperdine, I began coaching some triathletes for the Ironman® World Championship and other shorter races. It all happened quite serendipitously, with two of my closest friends, Scott Edwards and Mike Durkin, becoming my first triathletes. At the time, the "Big Four" were the guys to beat (Dave Scott, Mark Allen, Scott Tinley, and Scott Molina)—and Durkin beat two of them on occasion, Scott Tinley and Dave Scott. I would sometimes take part in the swim leg in relay races, but otherwise I travelled to almost every race with them in my capacity as coach and became a great student of the sport. This was an important era for triathlon: The sport was still in its infancy, but it was the birth of its professionalism. Events were growing in participation all the time, race directors were getting involved, and prize money was becoming more commonplace. I was gaining valuable experience and exposure, and my coaching career was officially under way. I travelled to Kona, Hawaii, for the 1985 Ironman World Championship, and like so many I was captivated by the race.

Back home in Los Angeles, a group of like-minded friends—Kevin Steele in particular—and I got together and created one of the area's first triathlon clubs:

Team Malibu. This subsequently led to my organizing and starting the Malibu Masters Swim Club. The program was attracting an increasing number of triathletes, so I was continuing to get a lot of exposure to endurance athletes of all ages and abilities. My extensive open-water experience was also proving invaluable. I was quickly coming to see how much most triathletes dreaded the prospect of the swim section of their race and how much they had to learn.

Although I thoroughly enjoyed my experience at Pepperdine, my own college swimming career had left me deeply unsatisfied. I was, at best, an insignificant swimmer, perhaps because of being thoroughly overtrained from the high weekly volume (80,000–100,000 yards). That was *de rigueur* back then. When my college swim career concluded in 1983, I rarely competed, but I wanted to continue to train and did so with the Palisades Masters under an extraordinary coach, Rick Goeden.

Throughout my swimming career, I swam with a number of coaches, but Goeden was one of the most influential. He taught me a great deal about how to interact with athletes and how to engage with all swimmers on the pool deck regardless of their fitness, speed, or ability. If you showed up to practice and had a willingness to learn and improve, you earned his attention. Although I might not have realized it at the time, the craft of coaching is as much about those tricks, subtleties, and nuances as it is about prescribing workouts.

Although I remained fully committed to swimming, after I had my freshly earned degree in business administration in hand, I was eager to figure out what was next. I first ventured into insurance and then banking, all the while continuing my swim training and learning from coaches.

The competitor in me could not lie dormant for too long. In 1988, I entered the Swim Around Manhattan, a 28.5-mile race that goes up the East River and down the Hudson. I knew putting a race like that on my calendar would motivate me to increase my training and return to competition. It worked; I raced nearly 30 ocean events up and down the California coast that summer in preparation for Manhattan and won most of them, with my wily, self-taught, open-water tactics. I could outsmart much younger, fitter swimmers with a specific, race-targeted training plan and open-water skill and strategy. However, deft maneuvers were not enough to seal victory at a race like Manhattan. Despite leading by almost a mile at one point, I faded to finish eighth. It was a lesson on the importance of nutrition for endurance athletes. Having forgotten my planned race nutrition, I covered those long miles around Manhattan on some electrolyte drink and half of a peach the captain of the support boat had donated to me from his lunchbox.

I was still working a sales position in the banking industry, but I now knew that coaching was my passion. As soon as I hit my sales target for the month, I would dedicate the rest of my time to brainstorming how I could viably make a living from swimming. While my banking coworkers buzzed around me, I sketched my proposed revenue stream on the backs of sales sheets. It comprised four things I wanted to do: own a swim team, organize events, own Speedo, and own a swimming magazine.

Within a year, I had achieved three of those goals, having bought *Swim Magazine*, taken over Southern California Aquatic Masters, and started the Great Beach Challenge Series. In 1995, I won a contract to develop a masters swim program at UCLA. I took it, and the program grew from zero to several hundred people in a relatively short space of time, becoming popular not only with masters swimmers but also triathletes. While coaching at UCLA, I struck up a friendship with Spitz, who swam laps there. He would later join some of my workouts and has been a supporter of many of my ventures over the years.

Life was overwhelmingly busy, and I was consistently working 80-hour weeks. In addition to coaching and co-owning *Swim Magazine*, I became co-publisher and chief operations officer (COO) of two more publications, *Swimming Technique* and *Swimming World*. With little hesitation, in 2006 I made a great decision: I quit anything not related to coaching. From then on that would become my sole focus. It was time to dedicate myself to my one true calling.

Up until 2006, I had been predominantly coaching masters swimmers, and during those formative years I was able to assist many adult athletes in achieving hundreds of accolades. I helped scores of swimmers earn top 10 national rankings, win national championship titles, and become world champions with national and world records. I even helped mentor and coach a few younger athletes, such as Lenny Krayzelburg, who would go on to win four Olympic gold medals, and Eva Fabian, who won gold at the 2010 FINA World Open-Water Swimming Championships.

Triathletes featured heavily in most of my masters programs, starting from the open-water swim workouts I held at Will Rogers Beach and then Manhattan Beach. Triathlon had been growing at a rapid rate since its inclusion in the 2000 Olympic Games. With an increasing number of professional triathletes moving to the Los Angeles area, I began running beach workouts from the Tower 26 lifeguard station in Santa Monica in 2009. These Wednesday morning sunrise workouts grew to regularly attract more than a hundred participants. Official Tower 26 pool workouts began a year later, and in no time at all there were a few hundred members, most actively competing in triathlon. The energy surrounding the sport was exciting. Typical triathletes race often and are keen to monitor progress, make improvements, and invest a lot into being their best selves. To succeed in the sport, they need the skills to perform in open water, my bailiwick. All of this resonated with my coaching philosophy, so I decided from that point forward I would focus on coaching triathletes.

I wanted the Tower 26® program not only to get athletes fit and race ready but also to help change their relationship with swimming. It was my experience that most triathletes viewed the swim portion of their race as something to survive. "I've just got to get to my bike," I would hear athlete after athlete say. Decades later, despite all of the advances made in the sport, my initial observations in the early 1980s still ring true. I wanted Tower 26 athletes standing on the start line of a race to feel ready to execute their best swim yet, to embrace the opportunity to compete, and to look forward to using all the skills they had learned with confidence and ease.

The Tower 26 swim workouts were born out of the specific demands of the sport at a time when few were doing this. Deck-ups, pace lines, sighting, and drafting were considered unusual when Tower 26 began, but these skills remain the cornerstone of our program today.

The program grew with each season. Professional triathletes from all over the world were coming to Los Angeles to tap into the magic of our program—some staying for two weeks, others for two years—as we worked with their respective coaches to help them become the best athletes they could be. The presence of these athletes at workouts was inspiring for all of the age-group athletes, too. I knew we were building something special. Tower 26 became a place where people came to swim but left with so much more than a workout. I hadn't just built a swim team but an extended family, with camaraderie, community, friendship, and loyalty at its core.

In recent years I wanted to extend the Tower 26 program to better reach athletes everywhere. Together with Jim Lubinski, I launched a triathlon swim podcast series, *Be Race Ready*. I hoped that we could cut through some of the noise in the triathlon community about what was required for successful triathlon swimming. It's been rewarding to use this opportunity to focus on the essentials and educate listeners in more than a hundred countries worldwide.

With a similar mindset, we created the Tower 26 subscription swim plan. Triathletes and open-water swimmers anywhere in the world can tap into my expertise and follow workouts, day after day, week after week, all season long. As a fully integrated triathlon service provider, we also offer triathlon coaching, bike trainer workouts, and track workouts.

Although my coaching philosophy has evolved since those early days, these core principles and values have guided me since that time and will continue to:

There are no shortcuts.

There are no secrets.

You have to show up *consistently,* with a positive attitude.

You must believe in yourself.

You must have a goal.

You must be patient.

You must apply yourself diligently in mind, body, and spirit.

You must be present and accountable.

As a coach, I am responsible for being prepared and providing a well-laid-out plan. Training sessions must be specific and meaningful, with an end result in mind and a mechanism to measure return or improvement. I also consider it my responsibility to encourage swimmers to learn from other coaches; after all, no coach has a monopoly on technique, training, or motivation. Humility is essential for coaches and athletes alike. The day you think you've made it—that will be your last best day.

Regardless of how competitive you set out to be, I believe that recreational swimming enthusiasts, masters swimmers, and triathletes can all be successful in an ambitious training environment. A less ambitious format only caters to the lowest common denominator. You might not be training to be the best athlete in the world or even compete in an event, but you will end up being the best athlete you can be.

Triathlon Swimming will equip you in all aspects, from training principles, workouts, and open-water skills to technique, equipment, and race preparation. We are all unique; no one person responds in the same way, but if you are willing to learn and work, I can help you swim faster than you may have ever thought possible.

1

An Introduction to Triathlon Swimming

TO THE UNTRAINED EYE, there might be little that differentiates traditional swimming from triathlon swimming, but the differences are important to understand. Under the broad umbrella of swimming, there are many specialties, including competitive age-group pool swimming, open-water racing, masters swimming, adventure open-water swimming, and triathlon swimming. Taking the training methodologies from one of these disciplines and blindly applying it to another is, at best, shortsighted and, at worst, a recipe for poor performance. But all too often coaches and athletes from one world step into another and offer advice and guidance that, however well intended, is not in the best interests of the athlete.

Relative to the open-water racer or the swimmer, the average triathlete has significantly less time for swimming—in fact, some age-group triathletes have just one to three hours a week to spend in the pool. This time is precious and must be used wisely to reap the greatest gains. Although it would make perfect sense for a pool swimmer to spend an hour a week practicing starts and turns, it would be foolish to give the triathlete a similar task. The closer we look at the demands of each discipline of swimming, the easier it is to see their nuances and specificities—and these must be respected and trained accordingly. There are enough differences, even between training for open-water swimming versus open-water swimming for triathlon, that I consider them two different sports.

When it comes to triathletes, *the single biggest factor to take into account is time*. With three sports to train for, strength training, and work and family commitments, athletes must be efficient. Although triathletes want to get the greatest bang for their buck from their training, they also want to become better athletes. In my view, four keys will unlock better triathlon swimming and improved performance:

1. **Get a proper training prescription.** This is where the greatest improvements lie for many athletes. Committing to a sensibly periodized program that develops endurance, speed, power, technique, open-water optimization, and recovery yields the greatest gains.
2. **Increase your training volume.** Most triathletes do not swim enough. I ask amateurs to commit to three swims a week, and pros even more.
3. **Improve your swim mechanics.** Triathlon swimmers tend to be well aware of the need to improve their swim mechanics, and they will even go so far as to spend an entire session each week working on this. For best results, technique work should be integrated into every workout.
4. **Be accountible.** Athletes step up their game if they have a coach overseeing their progress, be it in person or remotely. Being present at workouts and fully engaged in the process also leads to big returns.

If you can implement all four of these keys within a season, improvement and success will follow. If you are frustrated with stagnant seasons of no progress, this is how to break out of your plateau. To some extent, you might prioritize these objectives based on where you are in your progression as a swimmer. A novice with limited swim experience and major flaws in stroke mechanics would do well to focus on improving those mechanics first, but this wouldn't be at the expense of the other three keys.

Imagine you have taken years off from running, and you decide one day to go for a run. Unless you're superhuman, it's highly likely that within a few minutes of starting out, you'll feel extremely fatigued and be strongly considering walking or heading home. It's highly unlikely you'd return home and immediately Google running lessons, but for some reason, when people first start swimming, they seem to think that taking swim lessons will help their fitness return faster or that their fatigue is related to poor swim mechanics. There are certainly occasions when taking swim lessons could be valuable, but before considering them, let's first examine what you should get from a lesson:

▶ Some form of technical enhancement or stroke modification that will yield improvement.
▶ Simple feedback that you can take to the pool and apply.
▶ Quantifiable measurements that can be used as a point of comparison over time, such as stroke rate while swimming at race effort, stroke count (the number of strokes per length), and performance time over a specified distance.

Remember that you might not see any performance improvement to begin with, even if you do take swim lessons. This is why it's imperative to have some level of swim fitness before jumping into a lesson. You need to train your muscles and build the muscular endurance necessary in order to perform the basic stroke mechanics before attempting to change or improve them. If you can do the following skills, then swim instruction is not initially needed:

▶ You breathe to the side, keeping your head in the water rather than above it.
▶ Your arm stroke is an underwater propulsive movement, followed by your hand exiting the water and then returning to the entry point.

After you can do the basics, you need to practice them. Even if an athlete's stroke is inefficient, they need to build some specific muscular endurance before trying to make technical enhancements. Here's why: Your upper body needs to have the muscular strength and resilience to set up and pull the water repeatedly before you can do it with technical efficiency. Of course, an element of improvement is based on technical ≫

learning and understanding, but you need to be fit enough to effectively absorb and apply what you learn. This application resonates in all three sports, but it's greatest in swimming because of discomfort, fears, or negative experiences. A sense of comfort in the water must be established first, and building specific fitness makes that possible.

As a basic rule, before taking a swim lesson, I recommend at least three weeks of training, three to four sessions a week for 45–60 minutes per session, at varying efforts. This practice will put you in a better position to get the most from a swim lesson and absorb technical instruction.

Swim lessons, consultations, or video analysis can be very valuable, but do not assume you'll suddenly be able to swim faster. Weeks or months of work might be required before you can make meaningful performance improvements. Triathletes often want to join our Los Angeles program three weeks out from their first race, expecting to see magical gains from joining a workout. Although I would love to be able to make such promises, unfortunately I cannot—neither can any other coach out there. After you have taken a lesson, there must be a good feedback system in place to help you absorb and apply all that has been assessed, whether that comes from resubmitting videos or having a coach poolside to offer live feedback and instruction. It often takes several attempts at making changes before you actually nail them. Use videos of yourself swimming—this visual feedback makes it far easier to get back into the water and correct an error.

Most athletes looking for improved performance are preoccupied with technique and mechanics, thinking it will be a fast fix. Although this can be the case sometimes, it should not be the focal point. In fact, some triathletes have been conditioned to think that several months of drills will help them swim faster, but it really only makes them better drillers, not faster swimmers. Almost all novices seem to think that a swim lesson will contribute to some sort of performance magic, and they often want to start there, thinking it will yield the greatest gains. Let me fill you in on a secret: Technical improvements in swimming cannot take hold unless some degree of specific muscular endurance is in place. You need a basic swim endurance foundation before you can absorb technical modifications—and then those technical modifications must be trained. Improvements take time; there are no quick fixes!

It is still possible to swim exceptionally well with less-than-optimal stroke mechanics. We need only watch the Olympic Games to prove this point: World-class swimmers have flaws in technique, yet still break records and stand atop the podium. Their coaches know that time spent attempting textbook technique pales in comparison with smart implementation of the training volume and dosage. Let's take a closer look at all of the keys that contribute to improved performance.

GET A PROPER TRAINING PRESCRIPTION

Sensible periodized training—hitting the right types of workouts at the right time of the season—is the key to success in any sport, but because time is such a scarce commodity for triathletes, proper prescription becomes the all-important key to swimming improvement. I discovered relatively early in my coaching career that varying intensity within each workout is incredibly effective. Too often, I see athletes swimming long, slow, steady distances in preparation for their triathlon swim, but this does not prepare them for the swim start or the first 100–200 meters of the race. The body needs to be trained to swim hard at the start and then settle in. You need to practice in training what you plan to execute in racing, such as swimming hard at the start, finding clear water, remaining in control and not being at the mercy of adrenaline. Many athletes attempt to do things in races that they have not practiced, which never goes well.

I have also encountered triathletes who think if they can swim 10 × 100 at a 1:40 per 100 pace, they should simply train to build their load to 40 × 100, holding the same pace. They will likely have the endurance, but they are not going to swim faster on race day. All they have practiced is swimming farther at the same pace, not faster. Their ability to inject speed has not been trained.

This problem seems isolated to swim sessions because triathletes clearly know how to bike and run fast—I hear about their VO_2max bike and run workouts with regularity. Why not access the same intensity or speed in swimming? There is only one way to get faster—you must turn up the intensity. Here's an example of how

I weave this aspect of training into a workout for an advanced triathlete. This workout set of 25s hones top-end speed, and the pull recovery allows for a subtle inclusion of technique work—a great example of how we can combine different elements within a given workout.

SPEED + INTENSITY LEVEL 1 | Workout Set

20 × 25 at 90% effort with 0:10–0:15 rest
1 × 400 pull with snorkel, buoy, and ankle strap at 70% effort
Repeat for 3 rounds.
Level 2 MOD: 16 × 25 speed set, 400 pull recovery
Level 3 MOD: 14 × 25 speed set, 300 pull recovery
Level 4 MOD: 12 × 25 speed set, 300 pull recovery

To determine which level of workout is appropriate for you, see p. 32.

INCREASE YOUR TRAINING VOLUME

The average age-group triathlete has about two hours a week to dedicate to swim training, which just isn't enough. When triathletes join us at Tower 26, we ask them to increase swimming to three times a week. This usually represents a 50 percent increase; in my experience that's typically needed to make gains. We squeeze a lot of volume into those three sessions, too, so triathletes joining our program experience a sizeable increase in training distance, but within two to three weeks they grow accustomed to the new volume. It would never be advisable to increase volume so quickly with cycling or running because of risk of injury, but weight displacement in the water lowers the impact on the body.

IMPROVE YOUR SWIM MECHANICS

Acquiring better stroke mechanics and triathlon-specific technical knowledge can be a hugely time-consuming project. This time can be better spent working on more than just one component. Elements of improving stroke mechanics are woven into almost every session I prescribe, and I do this with three specific factors in mind: tautness, alignment, and propulsion (TAP®). I never focus exclusively on these factors, but they are built into warm-ups throughout the season. When combined with power, speed, endurance, and pulling, these factors help swimmers move toward better technique and fitness. Tautness, alignment, and propulsion underpin all of the technique work we do together. Because they build upon each other, they should be approached in a specific order.

Tautness

Tautness is the backbone of technique, upon which we build alignment and propulsion. When you are in the water, almost 90 percent of your body weight is displaced, so learning how to hold and move your body with some degree of tension—or tautness—is the first step to mastering better technique. Watch good swimmers, and you will see that they know how to hold their bodies as they swim—it is a learned skill, feeling, and posture. Regardless of how much power and propulsion you generate, if you are not taut in the water, you won't get the same return on your effort. In Chapter 3 we will work on tautness with a progression of drills using fins, snorkel, and a kickboard as well as vertical kicking. To gauge how taut you are in the water, consider these three touch points: the back of your head, your butt, and your heels. All three should be at the surface of the water at all times. All of the drills and cues I will give you are simply proprioception stimulation in water that teaches which muscles to use and how to activate them given the right tension.

Alignment

After you know how to hold your body with good posture in the water, it is time to progress to alignment. This is where the most problematic swim errors occur. As you move through the water, you want to maintain good alignment, that is, keep your body in a straight line from head to toe. As soon as misalignment happens, we see mistakes and compensations elsewhere in your stroke or body. Head positioning, breathing mechanics, body rotation, and hand entry all affect alignment for better or worse.

DRILLS WILL MAKE YOU A BETTER SWIMMER | Swim Myth

Of the many swim myths, one frustrates me more than most: the unfounded belief that drills will make you a better swimmer. The majority of triathletes I hear talking of or see executing certain drills simply do not have the technical foundation or fitness to perform them. Maybe they've read or listened to inexperienced coaches and uninformed authors. There are many credentialed triathlon coaches without swim coaching experience. With no understanding, they might prescribe drills that are too advanced or of little value to their athletes.

To really get the benefits from drills, you need a coach to be watching you. For a time-starved triathlete, time spent performing outdated or extremely advanced drills—especially without a coach's feedback—is futile. If the primary objective is to improve technique, this is a worthy pursuit, but let's be clear: There are better, more time-efficient ways to optimize technique and fitness.

The platform for all technical work is tautness, alignment, and propulsion. In the technical phase (October through December), this is a focal point. Throughout the rest of the year, the start of every workout still contains a technical element before we move into the training aspect of it. The bedrock for good performance is good mechanics, so not for one moment am I advocating ignoring this, but we must not focus on it at the expense of all else. There is a place for technical focus in every session, but as you will see in the workouts at the end of Chapter 4, my philosophy involves executing a bite-sized portion of a drill and then working that into the full stroke rather than doing endless and ineffective drills. We execute a drill and then immediately swim afterward because we want to become good swimmers, not good drillers.

Propulsion

I like to break the propulsive phase of the stroke into two parts: first, the hand and arm enter the water and extend forward and downward. You do not generate any propulsion during this part of the phase—your arm is simply entering the water and setting up to generate force. Next comes the propulsive phase: The arm has gone from being straight to having a slight bend at the elbow. You want enough tension in the hand and forearm to "grab" the water and hold on to it, driving your hand all the way back until it exits the water at the hip and propels the body forward. The arm recovers, the stroke begins again, and both parts have happened in less than a second.

Although there will likely always be passionate debate among coaches and athletes regarding which technical skills and drills are best, there are enough commonalities to outline general guidelines. Knowing these technical guidelines and approaching them methodically and systematically becomes crucial to both budding and seasoned triathletes' success. Making sure triathletes nail the fundamentals and do not get caught up in drills that are too advanced is the best service I can provide them with limited time. I like to remind athletes to keep it simple.

BE ACCOUNTABLE

Having a coach and being accountable is a guaranteed way to improve after proper prescription, increased training volume, and improved swim mechanics are in place. When you know you have someone watching, effort and commitment increase exponentially. From a purely technical perspective, having a coach poolside to observe stroke mechanics and deliver instant feedback often leads to significant gains. Other times it's as simple as knowing you must get to a workout at a specific time and day, which helps motivate you to hit a session you might never have accomplished alone. The real win happens when athletes feel accountable not only to their coach but also to their lane mates.

Being present (or mindful) at workouts goes hand in hand with accountability. For triathletes to get the most from each session, I expect them to show up with purpose, ready to give their full attention. As we have already outlined, triathletes have limited time to budget for swimming, so they need to work on technique at each of their sessions if they are to get the best return on their training investment. For me, this means paying attention to workout prescription as delivered by the coach and giving the best effort on any given day. It is something any athlete, regardless of speed, fitness, age, ability, or background can control. If you are focusing on exactly what you are doing in that moment, then you are fully engaged and giving yourself 100 percent to the process. Mindfulness is something I see in all of the successful athletes I have coached, past and present.

After a coach is on board with an athlete's goals and dreams, then together they can commit to working toward those objectives. From a coach's perspective, I cannot emphasize enough the importance of an athlete understanding that improvement won't happen overnight. Those who make the greatest gains are those willing to undertake the journey—no matter how long that might be—with a level head and ample patience. This approach is the very best an athlete can adopt.

Commit to all four of these keys—proper prescription, increased training volume, improved swim mechanics, and accountability—and you will become a better triathlon swimmer. At Tower 26 this promise comes with a money-back guarantee because if swimmers consistently attend our program, I have every confidence that their performance will improve. Many triathletes might do one or two of the above—for example, increase their mileage or try to improve their stroke—but the combination of all four really leads to overall gains.

THE ATTRIBUTE THAT LEADS TO ADAPTATION

When it comes to understanding training and adaptation, consistency is king. Although coaches will always differ on training methodologies, I don't think there's a coach on the planet who won't agree with the importance of *consistency*. So, what does this great word mean? By definition it is "conformity on the application of something, typically that which is necessary for the sake of logic, accuracy, or fairness," according to the *Oxford English Dictionary*. Conformity for us means committing to training, day after day, week after week. The best athletes (and I do not mean the fastest, but rather the most successful, with the greatest gains) understand the importance of consistency. You will have good days, bad days, and ordinary days, but the work must still be done regardless. This is simply the ebb and flow of training: We work hard, we get tired, the body adapts and recovers, and we repeat. The athlete must understand that fatigue is part of the process, as is having a bad workout and feeling like you're not getting anywhere yet. Being able to take a step back from these feelings, whether they are physical or emotional, is pivotal to understanding training. We cannot deviate from the path if we are to succeed; instead we want to see steady, consistent attendance and commitment.

When **BRAD AUSTIN** joined the Tower 26 program in 2012, shortly after moving to Los Angeles for a new job as an investment analyst, he had no swimming background. He only "knew how not to drown," although he was a distinguished runner as a 400m and 800m competitor at Georgetown University. After meeting him at a clinic I hosted on triathlon swimming technique, I would have pegged him to be a 1:30 Ironman swimmer—if he could have completed the swim!

Brad's finance career was always his primary focus, and it often meant he was clocking 60–80-hour workweeks. Nevertheless, he committed to swimming with us three times a week, every week, and he was impressively consistent, swimming twice each week at 5:45 a.m. before work and once each weekend. He was making steady gains, at first largely because of his newly acquired grasp of stroke mechanics and technique.

It wasn't long before he was giving some of the pro athletes a tough workout. He continued to learn and execute good mechanics, his training volume was increasing, and he was following the program meticulously, so his training prescription was also on point.

His first race as a Tower 26 athlete was Ironman St. George in 2012, at which he posted a 1:11 swim. He had been a member of the program for three months. Two years later, he not only qualified for Kona but also clocked a 60-minute swim there, taking more than 10 minutes off his personal record (and this time without a wet suit). A year later, in 2015 at Ironman Arizona, he took another 5 minutes off his best time, posting a 55-minute swim split on his way to a sub-nine-hour finish and victory in the competitive 25–29 age group.

Over the space of three seasons, Brad sliced more than 15 minutes off his Ironman swim time and took his 70.3 swim PR down to 25 minutes.

Brad Austin's story is triathlon swimming's rags-to-riches tale. His success came from a blend of the four keys—proper training prescription, increased volume, improved swim mechanics, and accountability.

In his words: "Committing to the program and consistently being exposed to great swimmers under the watchful eye of great coaches with an emphasis on proper technique allowed me to make consistent gains in the pool."

2

The Tower 26 Training Cycle

I ENCOURAGE ATHLETES TO GAIN an understanding of how a training cycle works, both over the period of a year and from week to week. It's often the case that athletes come to me because they are frustrated by their lack of improvement. They have endured long periods of plateau and are sometimes on the cusp of quitting altogether. When I inquire about the variation and content of their swim workouts, I typically find that swimmers suffering performance plateaus have been swimming without adequate variation in intensity or speed. They might swim once or twice a week, and it's usually the case that they dread their sessions. Performance plateaus also happen when athletes follow a plan that attempts to do too much in a very short period and lacks proper methodology—such as a 12-week "quick-fix" plan.

To improve as a triathlete swimmer, you need to train at all speeds and intensities and cover all aspects of fitness and performance: technique, endurance, speed, race preparation, and open-water skill building. Ignoring or not training any one of these elements means you will have a significant chink in your armor come race day, with limited acquired resources. Developing these skills takes time—definitely more than 12 weeks. Over a year of training with Tower 26, you will progress through several phases with specific objectives: technical phase, build phase, sharpening phase, open-water skill-building phase, and race-ready phase. Each phase lasts for a set number of weeks and features progression week after week. For example, in the first week of the build phase, the main set might be 2,000 meters, but by the sixth week an advanced triathlete will be swimming 4,000 meters, twice the volume.

Our Tower 26 season plan is rooted in specific planning and periodization, and nothing is left to chance. Over the 35 years I have been coaching, I have learned that this overall architecture is not only vital but also successful and empowers athletes to make the greatest gains possible in the small window of time they have available for swimming each week.

This program works for triathletes of all abilities. It has yielded unquestionable results, helping triathletes achieve countless PRs and goals they previously thought were unreachable. But that point deserves emphasis: *This is a season-long program—it is not offering you a quick fix or an injection of speed or intensity.* Many other triathlon plans are available, from 12-week generic programs that offer a one-size-fits-all approach to slightly more customized plans tailored to specific races. These are the antithesis of my methodology. Sustainable results come through consistency and frequency of race-specific training, skill building, technical manipulations, accountability, hard work, and dedication over the longer term.

In the northern hemisphere the race calendar culminates with the Ironman World Championship in Kona, Hawaii, in October, and this serves as the basis for my Tower 26 plan. The multiphase design takes athletes through the full season, delivering them to their A race in peak fitness. Although each of the phases has a focal point—be it technique, endurance, skill building, sharpening, or race preparation—there are aspects of all of these elements covered each week that may be weighted differently depending on the season's phase. Athletes can join our coaching program at any time of the year, but they will start at whatever phase we are currently in. Those athletes who happen to begin the program in mid-October, at the start of the technical phase, will have the luxury of following the program from start to finish, but rest assured that if you were to join in the spring or summer there is still plenty of technical work and guidance in the later phases.

TECHNICAL PHASE

This phase is about 10 weeks in duration and runs from mid-October until the end of the calendar year. The technical phase is intended to enhance technique and promote rest and rejuvenation after a full year of training and racing. With its low impact on the body, swimming is the perfect sport for facilitating recovery, so I like to use this time to give athletes some rest from the other two disciplines. Because this period coincides with the holiday season, it is a great opportunity to enjoy more time with family and friends.

Time spent in the water during this phase is focused primarily on technique, with the goal of understanding and establishing good stroke mechanics. I often refer to this period as triathlon swim school. Although I am not a huge advocate of traditional drills throughout the year—they are either too advanced or misdirected when unsupervised—this is the time when we build in plenty of technique work and master some of the fundamental concepts of stroke mechanics. With focused practice, athletes can improve their proprioceptive awareness of these technical requirements, that is, what it actually feels like to swim with good mechanics.

This technical period lays the kinetic platform and prepares you to absorb the training load, injury free, in the upcoming phase starting January 1.

BUILD PHASE

The build phase spans January through March or April and continues the technical work but primarily focuses on laying the endurance foundation for the year ahead. The work undertaken during this phase sets you up to perform well and execute your triathlon swimming goals later in the season. Training load, both volume and intensity, increases over this 13-week phase in three-week microcycles. Select training sets are repeated to gauge performance from one microcycle to the next, and the specific complexion of ongoing technical work will decrease as training load elevates. The focus shifts now to increasing volume instead of technique, although we still include some technique work in the warm-up and pre-main sets.

SHARPENING PHASE

After the higher training load of the build phase is banked, you are ready to move into the sharpening phase. This 13-week period includes preparation for 100- and 1,000-yard/meter time trials, used to gauge speed and endurance. The first time trial is done in early January; the second one is around late April or early May, and is used to measure progress for every athlete.

For returning athletes, I am looking for big jumps in performance over the previous year's test. If athletes have followed the program consistently, then we typically expect performance gains at this point in the season. Up until this point, our workouts might more closely mirror that of a traditional swim program but more focused to triathletes' needs given their limited time budget. Technique practice and awareness still play a significant role.

OPEN-WATER SKILL-BUILDING PHASE

The triathlete's world of swim training changes completely during our next phase, open-water skill building. Almost all triathlon swims take place in open water, so to capitalize on the base and speed work athletes have already completed, they need to be able to approach open-water swimming with confidence and skill. This six-week phase in April and May incorporates many essential open-water skills into pool workouts, such as deck-ups, drafting, sighting, pace lines, and pack swimming. Workout architecture changes again in this phase because athletes must get used to swimming in close proximity to others, as they will in a race, and must become familiar with the discomfort of these situations. In short, in this phase triathletes are now learning to be open-water swimmers and need to acquire the necessary skills.

It is important that athletes maintain dedicated emphasis on proper swim mechanics because the introduction of sighting and other open-water variables can and will depreciate swim form.

RACE-READY PHASE

The final stage is the longest and lasts four to five months, taking athletes all the way through to Kona in October. This is the heart of the racing season, and during this phase, everything should come together: The technique, endurance, and speed have been built and the open-water skills learned. From here, it is about consistent training and logging valuable open-water swim time.

Athletes in my program in Los Angeles undertake at least one ocean swim workout a week, our Wednesday morning swims from Tower 26 in Santa Monica. This is the A session—the foundation session of the week—and, depending on where we are in this phase, these workouts can be one to two hours in duration. We regularly see 100 to 200 people join these sessions, and I divide the group into subgroups based on speed. Of course, ocean conditions often contribute to how challenging the workout might be, but I expect the takeaway from these sessions to be confidence—in being able to deal with any variables nature might throw at us on race day. I want you to be a trained athlete, capable of showing up to any race anywhere in the world with the confidence and skills to stand on a start line ready for anything.

During the race-ready phase, it is not uncommon for athletes to be reducing their overall weekly swim volume because they are increasing time spent cycling and running. In terms of the triathlete's swimming, the base has been built, that is, specific muscular endurance and power, and some open-water skills developed from the pool. The focus is upon carrying these skills into open water, increasing navigational IQ and situational awareness, and further developing open-water confidence and racing acumen. Additionally, we build a lot of race-specific work into pool sessions, practicing race takeout speed and high frequency of sighting in almost all main sets. As an added bonus, I sometimes like to surprise swimmers to help prepare them for all eventualities that can occur on race day. The athletes might occasionally arrive on the pool deck during this phase expecting me to prescribe the warm-up, but I tell them they will be swimming a 20-minute time trial, and they have only five minutes of dry-land time to prepare for it. I find this a brilliant way to highlight the importance of race day warm-ups as well as prepare them mentally for events that can and will happen when they race. As a coach and keen observer of human behavior, I enjoy watching how different personalities respond to the challenge and perform.

To illustrate the different goals of each phase, the table at the end of the chapter shows how the architecture of a 10 × 100 meter set would change throughout the training cycle. Naturally, the overall training volume would also change over these phases: ballooning during the build phase, becoming very defined during the sharpening phase, introducing skill acquisition during the open-water skill-building phase, and then settling into highly race-specific work during the final, race-ready phase. But as we look at this workout set, it's clear that the prescription changes in each phase and even within phases as various skills are introduced and systems worked. This is the marriage of art and science in coaching, and it is where the absolute significance of proper training prescription comes into play. This isn't a blind prescription of "just go swim for an hour" or "go swim for 45 minutes in the ocean." It is periodized, it is deliberate and methodical, and it requires presence and consistency over at least a year.

This multistage plan has been devised to give athletes the biggest return on their training investment and help them extract the greatest value from their hard work. Periodization is vital, and the plan must be followed closely. In my experience, the biggest gains come from an athlete adhering to the Tower 26 plan for a two-year period. That allows enough time to learn how to build a season, and afterward an athlete can and should be able to self-coach if they desire.

Understanding that progress comes over time can often be the hardest part for an athlete to accept, especially with much shorter-term training plans and so-called quick fixes available. Patience is a virtue not all athletes are blessed with, and waiting for results can lead to frustration. Many athletes tend to focus on what is happening in the short-term: "What can I do now? What can I do this week? Which workout is my favorite pro athlete doing?" This only exacerbates the problem.

This is where a coach's perspective is particularly valuable. A good coach looks through a longer lens to help deliver you to the start line of your A race in peak condition, with a broad, versatile skill set to match your finely tuned fitness and confidence.

Canadian professional triathlete **RACHEL MCBRIDE** joined Tower 26's subscription program in spring 2017 in order to improve their swimming through more focused, specific work.

After a year or so, Rachel went from being a second-pack Ironman swimmer to a front-pack regular who led out of the water at Ironman Canada in 2018 with a 51-minute swim split. Rachel credits the change with taking them training from "mindless" to "mindful."

Rachel is a huge fan of the simple but focused approach to swimming, in which everything is broken down into manageable, easy-to-understand pieces and has applied this approach to other areas of life when faced with larger problems or difficulties in getting a job done.

Rachel is particularly fond of how we apply this approach to mechanics and technique, believing that tautness, alignment, and propulsion become more accessible when a triathlete is swimming mindfully—describing the process of figuring out how to maintain tautness as a lightbulb they were able to switch on with faster swimming.

Mindfulness has been huge for Rachel and has played a significant role in their success and improvement. Rachel is arguably one of the most present and focused athletes with whom I have worked.

"I never thought it was possible to make the gains I have since first joining Tower 26. Swimming is now an asset, not a liability for me, and I go into every race with confidence and a clear plan of how to execute my job," Rachel says.

TABLE 2.1. HOW TRAINING EVOLVES THROUGHOUT A SEASON

	Effort	Rest
TECHNICAL PHASE 10 × 100	▸ Gently progress effort every 2 repeats, reaching 80% effort by the last 2 sets.	0:20–0:30 between sets
BUILD PHASE 10 × 100	▸ 80% effort	0:05–0:20 between sets *During this 13-week phase, these rest intervals can and will vary based on the training protocols and stimulation needed. In fact, rest will increase to 0:45 on some sets.*
SHARPENING PHASE 10 × 100	▸ 85% effort when preparing for the 1000 m time trial and 90–95% effort when preparing for the 100 m time trial.	0:05–1:00 between each set *We have one specific goal in this phase: Prepare triathletes to swim their fastest times for 1000 and 100 yards/meters. There will be short and long rest intervals to meet both types of set demands.*
OPEN-WATER SKILL-BUILDING PHASE 10 × 100	▸ 70–85% effort. Lesser effort as skills are introduced; greater effort when skills are better mastered.	0:10–0:30 between each set, depending on the set's demands
RACE-READY PHASE 10 × 100	▸ 80–95% effort. Lesser effort when more skill-focused; greater effort when race-specific demands are trained.	0:30–0:40 between each set, depending on the set's demands

Note: Exertion (e.g., 80% effort) is further explained in Chapter 3. More detail on equipment is in Appendix A.

Equipment	Prescription
Fins, snorkel, and kickboard, use of which to be systematically reduced and then eliminated by the conclusion of the 10-week phase.	*50 kick/50 swim. Technical focus on tautness and alignment focal points.*
None	*All swimming with consistent effort while maintaining a narrow variance in time.*
Tempo trainer	*Set preparation for the 1000 m time trial will typically demand consistent effort output at 85% with narrow variance in time and a short rest interval. Set preparation for the 100 m time trial would demand rest periods within each 100. For example: 25/50/25 as follows: 25 with 0:05 rest, then 50 with 0:10 rest, and then the final 25. Rest between 100s would be significant.*
None	*As skills develop, the prescription evolves. Because sighting is the most important skill, these 100s would be executed with one to three sights per 25, that is, approximately eight sights per 100 or one sight every 10th stroke.*
Tempo trainer	*Dive in, and swim the first 50 at 90+% effort (race takeout effort), sighting three times per 25; swim second 50 at 80–85% effort, sighting once or twice every 25 while drafting off a buddy. Immediately deck-up at conclusion. Switch leaders each 100.*

3

Training

TRIATHLON SWIM TRAINING looks significantly different than that of cycling and run training in terms of complexity, duration, and intensity, and there are a number of valid reasons for this. During swim workouts, the intervals are often much shorter, and total workout time is shorter, too. Traditionally, some swim coaches have used shorter intervals so that they could give their athletes technical feedback more frequently. The fact that pools are 25 yards, 25 meters, or 50 meters in length lends itself to this type of frequent feedback. Because swimming is such a technical sport, being able to give plentiful feedback and instruction was deemed necessary. This played a part in why these coaches developed sessions that featured shorter reps and more frequent rest intervals, coupled with the fact that 90 percent of competitive swim events are approximately four minutes or shorter. This is quite unlike what we see triathletes doing when they train for cycling and running.

Swimming for shorter durations and with more frequent rest intervals means intensity can stay higher than when swimming continuously. In my coaching experience, I have found that triathletes can handle this type of higher intensity load in the pool far more readily than they can while cycling or running. I have enjoyed learning from bike and run coaches, experimenting with some of their favorite workouts, and transferring lessons from these to the pool. Conversely, there are some smart and successful triathlon coaches, such as Matt Dixon of Purple Patch Fitness and Brett Sutton of Trisutto, who have brought their swim coaching knowledge to triathlon, incorporating these intervals into their bike and run sessions with terrific success. Being open-minded and not caught in tradition can often lead to further optimizing training methodologies.

I believe shorter intervals also help to build fitness at the start of the training year, and we can then build up to longer intervals as the season progresses. Breaking the workload into shorter swim distances means we can ask athletes to train at a higher output. Shorter intervals also help incorporate technical work, such as improving tautness, so there are technical benefits to this approach, too. The load for athletes in the pool can be higher, yet the recovery rate is faster, so the formula yields improvement without undue cumulative fatigue. The ocean swim workouts in Santa Monica are a great example of this: Each loop might be five to nine minutes in duration, and intensity during these swims is often very high, but there are plenty of opportunities for rest and recovery between each repeat. As a result, the gains from these race-specific sessions are significantly greater than if we were to just swim at a steady aerobic pace for the duration of the workout.

WORKOUT ARCHITECTURE

There are typically three segments to every workout, and they rarely change: warm-up, pre-main set, and main set. Of course, the complexity and duration of these will vary depending on the training phase we are in, but they are the staples. As we progress through a season of training, the architecture of a workout will be dictated by the demands and focus of that phase. In the technical phase, for example, we would complete a longer warm-up than during the race-ready phase.

Warm-Up

The warm-up is an integral part of any workout and is designed to activate the body and prepare you for the workout ahead. Triathletes can often be tight or tired from previous sessions, so the warm-up often serves as a way to loosen the body and reduce the negative impact of a training hangover. We also want to minimize the risk of injury and maximize the value of the upcoming main set and the workout's key purpose.

Pre-Main Set

During this part of the workout, with a focus on stroke mechanics and technique, we begin to carefully elevate heart rate and get the athletes' bodies prepared for the main set to come. This section of the workout can be longer in duration during the technical phase, when there is a greater focus on executing drills. Over the course of this phase, we will build upon skills learned and incorporate these into the main set. During the technical phase, the main set will not be as long. Effort is lower than later in the year because the key objectives of this phase are recovery and technical enhancements.

Main Set

This is the key section of the workout and the part from which we look to extract the greatest training value. During the build phase, the main set becomes much longer in duration because we aim to build muscular endurance and power, and greater emphasis is placed on the main set. Over the course of the 13-week build phase, we will build on the main set in three-week microcycles so that as the sets and volume increase, intensity and distance do, too. This means the warm-up decreases slightly, especially compared to the technical phase.

During the sharpening phase, the complexity of the main set changes again because the workload becomes highly specific to swimming fast 100- and 1,000-yard/meter time trials. At this stage, workout structure becomes similar to a non-triathlete swimmer's regimen, building in specific speed and pace work.

The main set changes again when we hit the open-water skill-building phase. During the pre-main set, we introduce all the new technical elements and skills inherent in open-water swimming. These include deck-ups, pace lining, sighting, drafting, and pack swimming. At our program in Los Angeles, we hone all of these skills in the pool before trying them in open water. Swimmers need to get comfortable being in close proximity to—and often experiencing a lot of contact with—other athletes. These skills are initially introduced and developed in the pre-main set, when intensity is lower, and then carried forward into the main set, when intensity and workload are higher.

The complexity of the main set will change again when we reach the race-ready phase. Warm-ups shrink in time and duration and will often mimic that of a race day warm-up. All of the open-water skills we have been practicing in the preceding phase are built into main sets. For example, a main set might consist of 10 × 200 yards or meters, each one from a dive with a fast 50 at race takeout speed, multiple sightings every lap, and a fast finish and deck-up at the end. Pace lining or drafting can be incorporated into these swims, too.

Cooldowns

I am not a huge advocate of long, dedicated cooldowns, unless done with additional purpose, because our job with triathletes is to optimize their training time. For me, part of optimizing a workout might mean ending the session with a pull set so that some technical work is integrated into easier swimming. During these pull sets, effort rarely goes above 70–75 percent, and the focus is on technique, using a buoy and band as well as a snorkel. I see this as a great opportunity to work on stroke mechanics and detox athletes' bodies from the workload just undertaken. This also prepares your body to more effectively absorb its next training session. If a workout has involved extended periods at a higher effort (e.g., 90 percent effort or higher for more than 15–20 minutes), then I will prescribe a specific cooldown because your body needs and wants that time to detox. The cooldown would typically still be short in duration and pulling based.

ARCHITECTURE OF A TRAINING WEEK

I prioritize weekly sessions, labeling them A, B, or C workouts. I would expect a pro athlete to hit all of the workouts, but age-groupers should hit the A session first and the others only if time allows. During the race-ready phase, the open-water swim is always the priority, and if athletes can hit only one workout a week this is it. Even when a workout is labeled B or C, and therefore assumes less importance, crucial ingredients are contained in all of the sessions. Real example: Athletes swim three times a week—two A sessions on Tuesday and Thursday and then a B session on Saturday or Sunday. They miss an A session during the week because of travel, sickness, or family commitments so would then substitute the weekend's B session with the missed A session. The priority is fitting in the two A sessions each week.

Let's take a closer look at how the workout architecture plays out in this A-priority session, fondly known as the "Mambo" (a nickname given to me by Greg Bonan, *Baywatch* producer, based on my once-heavier Caribbean accent). This session is a staple feature in our build phase. It is a set that develops endurance, power, varying pacing skills, and mental fortitude. When we first do this set, we usually start with four to five rounds, depending on your ability level, and progress to eight rounds (for the faster swimmers) by the end of the phase.

The Mambo set is a perfect example of a benchmark set, or A-priority workout, repeated during the course of a phase or the year to highlight and map performance gains. We can train and train, but if there are no opportunities for assessing improvements, then we are often operating in the dark. In addition to sets such as the Mambo, the greatest opportunity we have for this type of assessment are our 100- and 1,000-yard/meter time trials, which for the Los Angeles–based swimmers are in January and April. Any athlete joining our online program is asked to complete the 100- and 1,000-yard/meter time trials within their first week of subscription.

These benchmark swims provide objective feedback and data on your current swimming level and how much you have improved. Time trials are yardsticks against which you can compare performance over a period of weeks, months, or

THE "MAMBO," A-PRIORITY | Workout

WARM-UP

10:00 of easy, fluid swimming

Not a hard stroke is taken. Depending on fitness and ability, this could be 400–800 yards/meters.

PRE-MAIN SET

8 × 100 as 50 kick/50 swim, with fins and a snorkel, progressing effort gradually with every two 100s from easy to Ironman effort

5:00 swim, integrating the technical elements executed in the prior set

We want to see a progression of heart rate here while we focus on stroke mechanics. This technical work could take 15–20 minutes, so we are now almost 30 minutes into the workout. Your body is warmed up and ready to absorb the main workload. We would rarely begin the main set without this type of progression unless we were in the race-ready phase.

MAIN SET

4 × 100 as follows: 100 at 70% effort, 100 at 70.3 pace, 100 at 70% effort, 100 fast

Repeat effort pattern for several rounds, with total number of rounds dependent on the phase or time of the season and one's ability level (see below). As you progress through the rounds you add 100 to that second swim (at 70.3 pace), so it would look like this:

Round 1: 100 easy, 100 at 70.3 pace, 100 easy, 100 fast

Round 2: 100 easy, 200 at 70.3 pace, 100 easy, 100 fast

Round 3: 100 easy, 300 at 70.3 pace, 100 easy, 100 fast

Round 4: 100 easy, 400 at 70.3 pace, 100 easy, 100 fast, and so on . . .

The intervals are set up to allow about 0:10 rest on the 70% effort (easy) swims, 0:10 rest per 100 on the 70.3 pace efforts, and 0:15 rest on the fast swims. Not as much rest is needed after the fast swims because the 70% effort that follows allows for active recovery, which has a great training effect.

Level 1 athletes: Start at 5 rounds and build throughout the season to 8 rounds.

Level 2 athletes: Start at 4 or 5 rounds and build throughout the season to 7 rounds.

Level 3 athletes: Start at 4 rounds and build throughout the season to 6 rounds.

Level 4 athletes: Start at 3 or 4 rounds and build throughout the season to 6 rounds.

COOLDOWN

Relaxed, easy swimming for a few minutes

years. If you have consistently progressed through the program, then you should be seeing improvements. If you aren't seeing gains, then we need to look at why.

We cannot take shortcuts or expedite adaptation; it takes place as we work hard, learn, recover, and bounce back. Adaptation typically takes place over a three-week period, or 10 swims. For example, if you repeat a skill 10 times for a predetermined duration over this three-week period, you will usually start seeing improvement. It won't happen in just one or two workouts; it takes repeated patience and commitment, but in my experience, almost everyone experiences some change in this time frame. Elite athletes can sometimes be ahead of the curve, and those with a limited athletic background might need a little longer, but the good news is that adaptation is within reach.

Key swim sessions should come ahead of, and not on the heels of, major run or bike workouts. This isn't just me coming at it from a swim perspective only; I'm looking at it in terms of what will lead to the greatest overall gains for athletes across all three sports. Simply put, running loves swimming, and swimming hates running. Get it wrong at your peril! By this, I mean that swimming after a run workout will expedite your recovery from that run and help loosen and elongate your muscles. It promotes recovery for your next workout, and many athletes like to swim after a long, hard run, if only for a short duration. However, the same cannot be said of what running before a key swim workout does for swimming: It can compromise that session. For this reason, it is important to think about where in your training week your key workouts are placed. I would not want to see an athlete do a key bike or run workout on a Wednesday evening and then attempt a key swim workout early Thursday. The odds increase significantly that the Thursday swim will be compromised. As often as possible, place the essential swim training at the start of your day. This can often be a balancing act when training in extremely hot and humid conditions and vying to complete all key workouts before temperatures become unbearable.

MEASURING EXERTION

I have always found that the key to successful training is not overcomplicating it. For example, I rarely use the word *threshold* because it is just too nebulous a word. We have an aerobic and an anaerobic threshold, so to use the word interchangeably leads only to confusion for athletes, as far as I have experienced. Additionally, threshold can have differing interpretations within each specific sport, depending on how coaches within that sport use the word, which then influences how their athletes interpret it. I prefer to deliver workouts in terms of percentage effort, and I ask athletes to learn to do this: Match an effort level to a feeling and to a performance time or yield. This is not easy and takes time, patience, and learning. In an age when many athletes have data coming at them from their wrist and their cell phone every moment, asking an athlete to learn the art of understanding biofeedback can be a tough one, but I stand by it. I want you to develop an understanding that a certain output yields a certain time and gives you a certain feeling.

As you can imagine, mindfulness is the centerpiece of experiencing this feeling. Attempting to do this without being 100 percent engaged in what you are doing at best slows the process and at worst leads to frustration. You need to know what 80 percent effort feels like and what time that yields for a 100-yard/meter repeat. You also need to recognize that if you take only one of these factors in isolation (e.g., time), without due regard to effort level or feeling, then you can fall short. For example, let's say for a set of 10 × 100 meters with 10 seconds rest at 80 percent effort, you typically average 1:30, but during your most recent workout you hit 1:33 to 1:35. If you consider only the times, this might lead to frustration: "Why am I swimming slower?" "What is wrong?" But here the feeling of the effort on that given day becomes important. You might have still been swimming at 80 percent effort, but on this day, you were particularly fatigued or had had a stressful week at work or were sleep deprived. Taking these things into consideration is key for progress and motivation. If you were to look only at time rather than combine it with feeling and effort, you would be missing important pieces of the puzzle.

Learning to gauge effort and feeling is probably the most important skill to develop for racing. If you can learn what 80–85 percent effort feels like in training, you can carry this over to race day, and for many athletes, this is when the real breakthrough occurs. Canadian pro triathlete Rachel McBride is a great example of this. Prior to working with Tower 26, she said she was not aware of marrying a certain percentage of effort to a certain feeling. After many months of mindful hard work with us, she developed this skill, and it led to her making huge gains. In the early stages of the swim at Ironman Canada in 2018, she found herself on the feet of some well-known front-pack swimmers. Ordinarily, she might have thought: "This is good, wow, I'm in a good position, I'm swimming with X and Y athlete," but instead she checked in with herself and had the experience of her training with which she could compare. She realized she was swimming way below 80 percent effort. She put in a push and swam around and away from those front-pack swimmers to lead out of the water in 51 minutes. This was not only a huge PR for her but perhaps more significantly a huge confidence boost and mental breakthrough. She swam away from competitors she had never before swum close to and beat them out of the water by a couple of minutes, helping to set up a great race for her.

Teaching athletes to swim at different intensities and know how these efforts feel are central parts of my training methodology. During a workout, you might find yourself swimming at a number of different effort levels, and I like varying intensities like this. It is very easy and incredibly tempting for some athletes to swim at one effort level for an entire session, much as you might during a long bike or run workout. But doing this in the pool leads to shortfalls in performance: You need to know how to swim at 90 percent effort, and you need to learn to tolerate the discomfort that brings. Varying intensity in this way means that come race day you have a number of different gears at your disposal, and you are well prepared to execute a great swim. In short, you are race ready.

WORKOUT LEVELS

Just as you would find your appropriate lane at a masters class based on your pace, we scale workouts based on pace. There are four levels, and regardless of which level you are in, your workout will deliver quality sets that lead to adaptation. Use Table 3.1 to determine the appropriate level.

I have found that quite often novices who inquire about joining the Tower 26 program think it is only for professionals or elite age-groupers, or they think: "I'm not good enough." I can assure you that we have swimmers of all speeds and abilities. In fact, Level 1 swimmers only make up around 8 percent of our program, both online and in Los Angeles. There is a misnomer that our program has a high percentage of professionals, perhaps in part because a number of professional athletes joined the program who went on to make great gains with their swimming, and this often makes headlines. In fact, at Tower 26 the professional and elite age-group athletes are in the minority. About 25 percent of swimmers in our program are Level 2, 33 percent are Level 3, and 34 percent are Level 4, the largest cohort. I enjoy telling this to newcomers who say they are intimidated. Please set your fears aside; you will be in good company! More than two-thirds of the people in our program are posting upward of 37 minutes for their 70.3 swim.

TABLE 3.1. PACE-BASED LEVELS FOR WORKOUTS

	100 yd.	100 m	70.3	Ironman
LEVEL 1 ▸	< 1:15	< 1:25	< 28:00	< 58:00
LEVEL 2 ▸	1:15–1:29	1:25–1:39	28:00–34:59	58:00–1:10:59
LEVEL 3 ▸	1:30–1:49	1:40–1:59	35:00–39:59	1:11:00–1:29:59
LEVEL 4 ▸	1:50+	2:00+	40:00+	1:30:00+

Former musician and full-time mom **CHRISTELLE BALESTRA** acquiesced to her husband Christophe's requests for her to join him in the program in 2016. Up until that time, she was swimming solo in a lane next to the group workouts, feeling too intimidated to actually take part. She considered herself a novice, having learned to swim at age 39. With a busy family schedule, she averages three swims a week.

As a former violin and viola teacher who spent countless hours practicing during her formative years, she is no stranger to hard work, commitment, and consistency and appreciates how important those are in making improvements. Even so, the gains Christelle has made are impressive. In December 2016 her 70.3 swim time was 41 minutes. At 70.3 Oceanside in April 2017, she swam 39:36, and a year later at that same race she clocked 36:58. She then lowered this even further at 70.3 Santa Cruz in September 2018, posting a 33-minute swim split.

Christelle attributes her improvements to consistency. She never skips a swim and uses her training as a classical musician to focus on the task at hand.

4

Technique

STROKE TECHNIQUE IS HINDERED by some common flaws. Identifying and addressing these flaws can be a complex process, but I have developed an approach to teaching technique that yields tangible results. I tackle stroke technique in a three-step process in order of priority: First you'll master tautness, then alignment, and then propulsion. Only after you have grasped the concept and feeling of tautness can you progress to alignment and then propulsion. Swim technique and mechanics are often overwhelming, especially for athletes learning to swim later in life, but if you approach the goal of improving technique in this order, you will be able to absorb maximum knowledge with minimal confusion and get the biggest return on your time invested.

TAUTNESS

Optimal swim technique for triathletes starts with tautness. Consider the difference between an uncooked and a cooked spaghetti noodle. Left uncooked, the noodle is taut and does not flex much; after cooking, it is soft and limber. When we swim, we want to hold our bodies with just the right amount of muscular tension, or tautness. Too many swimmers "noodle" their way down the pool. Developing tautness, or proper structural integrity, takes time.

For new swimmers, adjusting to how their body feels in the water can be the hardest part. More than 90 percent of your body weight is displaced when you are in water, which creates an unfamiliar sense of weightlessness. You have a newfound body weight and very little awareness of what your body is doing and how best to move it, that is, a lack of proprioception. Accomplished swimmers learn how to hold their bodies in the water with great posture and tautness through the appropriate amount of muscular tension. As you build awareness and learn more about stroke mechanics, you can develop this ability.

My step-by-step process for achieving tautness involves swimming with a snorkel while kicking, then swimming with a kickboard and fins, with some vertical kicking as well as some fast swimming. At Tower 26 we dedicate three to four weeks during the technical phase to training tautness before progressing to alignment-specific work. Tautness training is included in workouts year-round because it is

---

Excessive movement of the head is often the biggest cause of problems with stroke mechanics and technique, so we use a **FRONT-MOUNTED SNORKEL** to help keep the head stationary. While you are wearing a snorkel, you have no reason to turn your head to breathe, which enables you to focus entirely on your stroke. We follow this mantra: no lifting, no tilting, no tucking. Maintain a fixed, neutral head position with the water line at the center-top of the head when in the horizontal swim position. Keeping your head neutral enables you to break down the stroke into bite-sized pieces and just focus on single elements. The primary focus while wearing a snorkel is alignment, where most issues with stroke mechanics occur. When keeping the head absolutely still, you can focus entirely on the alignment of your head, chest, hips, butt, and feet.

Unlike many other technical teaching tools, using a front-mounted snorkel will take some getting used to for most swimmers. You need to inhale and exhale solely through your mouth or you will end up taking in water through your nose. Allow yourself 10 sessions to build familiarity.

---

such a critical component of good technique, and especially because it is the first technical element to break down when fatigued. It can always be further honed.

To understand and "feel" tautness, you have to know how to kick while stabilizing the upper body. When it comes to swimming for triathlon, I am not a great proponent of kicking. When it comes to training tautness, we are not kicking for propulsion or improved kicking, although both are possible by-products of the effort. We are kicking to learn optimal posture.

10-Step Drill Progression to Achieve Tautness
Step 1: Kicking with a kickboard, a front-mounted snorkel, and fins

Hold the kickboard at its base, with your arms outstretched and your biceps squeezing your ears. Make yourself as long as possible. Hold your head in a neutral position, with your nose pointing to the bottom of the pool.

There are three important touch points, all of which should be at the surface of the water: the back of your head, butt, and heels. As you kick, be aware of whether your upper body is rocking—your main objective is to stabilize it by engaging your core. I refer to that point where you have the right amount of tension without being stiff as being "athletically relaxed." We cover short distances doing this, perhaps 12 × 25 yards/meters with 0:20 rest.

Step 2: Kicking with snorkel and fins, arms outstretched and thumbs interlaced

Put the kickboard away, and stretch your arms out in front of you, thumbs inter-laced, your biceps squeezing your ears. Kick with an elongated body.

Step 3: Kicking with snorkel and kickboard only

Removing the fins, now use just the snorkel and kickboard, still focusing on mini-mizing the rocking of your upper body. For poor kickers, kicking without fins sends a destabilizing vibration up the body, causing greater wobbling. A stable torso acts like a harness.

Step 4: Kicking with a snorkel only

Now use the snorkel, but swim without a kickboard or fins. Your arms are out-stretched in front of you, thumbs interlaced, biceps squeezing your ears as you kick with an elongated body. By now you will be building your proprioceptive awareness.

• • •

These first four steps have focused on teaching partial body and torso awareness, thereby manufacturing tautness. For total body awareness, it is essential to prac-tice kicking on your back.

Step 5: Kicking with fins while on your back

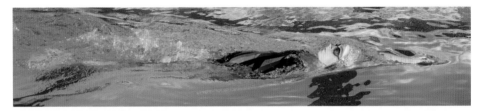

Hold your arms fully outstretched above your head, with the back of your hand resting on the water's surface, biceps still squeezing your ears tightly, front of hips at the surface of the water, tips of the fins kissing the water's surface as you use a standard freestyle kick.

Ultimately, we progress to doing this without fins. Fins are a tool to help you learn more quickly. Kicking without fins comes after familiarity is achieved.

Step 6: Vertical kicking

This is the all-important step to learn excellent body posture and awareness. In deeper water, hold your body pencil straight as you kick from the hip with a small bend of the knee. It is very easy to try to kick from the knee only, but this creates frontal drag and places a big demand on the quads, which you want to keep as fresh as possible for cycling and running. Make sure the kicking movement starts from your hips. Hold your hands out to your sides, not in front of your shoulders. Execution of this drill depends on good alignment and an efficient kick. Avoid

| CORRECT | INCORRECT | INCORRECT |

Avoid bending at your waist or allowing any trace of wobble in your torso.

bending at your waist or allowing any trace of wobble in your torso. Maintain a fixed-head position—don't let it drop or lean backward. Everything from head to toe must be taut and aligned to successfully execute this drill. Ask a training buddy or friend to check your posture or take a video. It can often feel like you're doing it correctly, but when you watch footage you can see your body is not yet in a straight line.

After you have learned how to vertically kick, graduate to raising your arms higher so that your elbows rest on the water, and then eventually fully extend them above your head.

Step 7: Perfect push-offs

Pushing off the wall is not an option in open water, but in pool swimming every push off the wall is a perfect opportunity to reset tautness and posture. Use your turns to uncoil and execute big, powerful push-offs from the walls. Make the most of this in the first few swim strokes. Postural integrity typically starts depreciating after those first few strokes, but if you're swimming in a 25-yard or 25-meter pool, the wall will be there soon enough, giving you another opportunity to reset.

Step 8: Fast swimming

High-intensity swimming stimulates tautness. If I ask you to sprint for 10–15 seconds, I can guarantee you will engage greater muscular tension to try to access maximum speed. We will keep these efforts short, no more than 25 yards/meters. Fast swimming is essential to learning tautness.

■ ■ ■

For the final two steps to achieving tautness, you will need a partner. During these exercises, you will learn to activate and engage all of the necessary stabilizing muscles to maintain balance. The engagement of these muscles is essential to maintaining proper posture when you swim, especially in a highly dynamic environment such as open water.

Step 9: Stabilization and core activation on dry land

By applying force to your shoulders, hips, chest, and back, you can learn how to activate the core stabilizers in your body and better maintain tautness in the water. Do this as a pre-workout drill to set yourself up with great posture. Be sure to remember exactly how this feels on land, and keep this feeling at the top of your mind when swimming, especially when you become fatigued. Holding this body tension will help your body position.

Stand stationary and relaxed, with your arms at your sides. Have your partner push your shoulder with gentle to moderate force. Engage your core and stabilizing muscles to counter the force, and hold your position. Repeat the drill on the opposite shoulder.

Have your partner push you with gentle to moderate force on your hip, and again engage your core to remain stable. Repeat on the opposite hip.

Have your partner push you with gentle to moderate force on your upper back between your shoulders. Again engage your core to remain stable. Repeat the drill on the chest.

Now you will move this drill into the water, and your partner will apply force to your shoulders, hips, and knees as you are stationary kicking.

Step 10: Stabilization and core activation in the water

Use a snorkel to keep your head in a neutral position, with your nose pointing to the bottom of the pool. Hold on to the lane line or pool wall, and with your arms outstretched, start kicking. Keep a long, taut body with a straight spine, and be mindful of the three touch points at the water's surface: your head, butt, and heels.

Have your partner push on your shoulder with gentle to moderate force. Engage your core and stabilizing muscles to maintain your taut position without being destabilized or moved off center. Repeat on the opposite shoulder.

Have your partner push on your hip with gentle to moderate force. Engage your core and stabilizing muscles to counter the force. Repeat on the opposite hip.

Finally, have your partner push on your upper back between your shoulder blades with gentle to moderate force. Engage your core and stabilizing muscles to counter the force.

• • •

Most swimmers need to dedicate several weeks to the tautness progression. Adaptation takes a minimum of three weeks or 10 sessions—that is, three to four times a week for three successive weeks. Be present in the execution of every step, carefully building one upon the other.

TAUTNESS | Keys

- ▸ Maintain a fixed head position. Keep the water line at the center-top of your head. Eyes should be looking down, not forward.
- ▸ Focus on staying as long as possible with proper posture.
- ▸ Keep the back of your head, butt, and heels at the surface of the water. Check in on where these touch points are every 10 seconds or several times per 25 yards/meters.
- ▸ For all prone kicking drills, keep your face in the water with your nose pointing toward the bottom of the pool. This facilitates stabilization and good body position.
- ▸ Minimize torso movement when kicking. Engage your stabilizing core muscles.
- ▸ Maintain a narrow kick, no wider than your shoulders.
- ▸ Kick from the hips.
- ▸ Mind your feet when you kick. Keep your toes pointed, feet turned inward, and big toes almost touching as they pass by each other.

Stretch cords

Warm-up: 600 easy swim

WARM-UP/TAUTNESS TECHNICAL

1 × 800 as 100 kick/100 swim continuous with fins

Kick on your back, arms outstretched overhead, thumbs interlaced, palms facing up.

Stationary head position, stable upper body, and three touch points with the surface (head, butt, and tips of fins).

8 × 50 as 25 kick/25 swim with snorkel (no fins) progressive effort with 0:15 rest

Progress effort to 80–85% by the fourth 50, and then hold that effort for the remaining 50s.

Thumbs interlaced and arms fully outstretched, arms by your ears, and palms facing down. Maintain stable torso, no wobbling. Three touch points with the surface: head, butt, heels.

8 × 0:15 vertical kicking with 0:20 rest

Keep your body in a straight line, hips stacked over feet, shoulders over hips, head over shoulders. Fingertips are above the surface of the water, hands in line with shoulders. Maintain upright position with a small, fast kick, big toes turned slightly inward.

Swim 10:00 at 70% effort with snorkel

Execute the three touch points (back of the head, butt, heels) and excellent body posture.

MAIN SET

8 × 25 swim with snorkel and kickboard (no fins), progressive effort with 0:20 rest

Progress effort until the fourth 25 is fast, and sustain for the remaining 25s.

Three touch points, stable torso, stationary head.

8 × 25 fast on 0:30

Fast swims force proper taut body posture. No equipment.

Access maximum power and propulsion as quickly as possible. Kicking should be narrow, with minimal knee bend, pointed toes, and elevated legs.

1 × 200 at 70% effort with 0:30 rest

Execute perfect wall push-offs to stimulate tautness at the start of each length.

Continue the tautness achieved from the push-off throughout the entire length. This is harder to do when swimming at 70% effort.

Stretch cords

Warm-up: 500 easy swim

WARM-UP/TAUTNESS TECHNICAL

1 × 800 as 100 kick/100 swim continuous with fins

Kick on your back, arms outstretched overhead, thumbs interlaced, palms facing up.

*Stationary head position, stable upper body, and three touch points with the surface
(head, butt, and tips of fins).*

8 × 50 as 25 kick/25 swim with snorkel (no fins) progressive effort with 0:15 rest

Progress effort to 80–85% by the fourth 50, and then hold that effort for the remaining 50s.

*Thumbs interlaced and arms fully outstretched, arms by your ears, and palms facing down.
Maintain stable torso, no wobbling. Three touch points with the surface: head, butt, heels.*

8 × 0:15 vertical kicking with 0:20 rest

*Keep your body in a straight line, hips stacked over feet, shoulders over hips, head over shoulders.
Fingertips are above the surface of the water, hands in line with shoulders.
Maintain upright body position with a small, fast kick, big toes turned slightly inward.*

Swim 10:00 at 70% effort with snorkel

Execute the three touch points (back of the head, butt, heels) and excellent body posture.

MAIN SET

8 × 25 kick with snorkel and kickboard (no fins) progressive effort with 0:20 rest

Progress effort until the fourth 25 is fast, and sustain that effort for the remaining 25s.

Three touch points, stable torso, and stationary head.

8 × 25 swim fast on 0:30

Fast swims force proper taut body posture. No equipment.

*Access maximum power and propulsion as quickly as possible. Kicking should be narrow,
with minimal knee bend, pointed toes, and elevated legs.*

1 × 200 swim at 70% effort with 0:30 rest

Execute perfect wall push-offs to stimulate tautness at the start of each length

*Continue the tautness achieved from the push-off throughout the entire length.
This is harder to do when swimming at 70% effort.*

TAUTNESS LEVEL 3 | Workout

Stretch cords

Warm-up: 450 easy swim

WARM-UP/TAUTNESS TECHNICAL

1 × 700 as 100 kick/100 swim continuous with fins

Kick on your back, arms outstretched overhead, thumbs interlaced, palms facing up.

Stationary head position, stable upper body, and three touch points with the surface (head, butt, and tips of fins).

7 × 50 as 25 kick/25 swim with snorkel (no fins) progressive effort with 0:15 rest

Progress effort to 80–85% by the fourth 50, and then hold that effort for the remaining 50s.

Thumbs interlaced and arms fully outstretched, arms by your ears, and palms facing down. Maintain stable torso, no wobbling. Three touch points with the surface: head, butt, heels.

8 × 0:15 vertical kicking with 0:20 rest

Keep your body in a straight line, hips stacked over feet, shoulders over hips, head over shoulders. Fingertips are above the surface of the water, hands in line with shoulders. Maintain upright body position with a small, fast kick, big toes turned slightly inward.

Swim 10:00 at 70% effort with snorkel

Execute the three touch points (back of the head, butt, heels) and excellent body posture.

MAIN SET

6 × 25 swim with snorkel and kickboard (no fins) progressive effort with 0:20 rest

Progress effort until the fourth 25 is fast, and sustain that effort for the remaining 25s.

Three touch points, stable torso, and stationary head.

8 × 25 swim fast on 0:30

Fast swims force proper taut body posture. No equipment.

Access maximum power and propulsion as quickly as possible. Kicking should be narrow, with minimal knee bend, pointed toes, and elevated legs.

1 × 150 at 70% effort with 0:30 rest

Execute perfect wall push-offs to stimulate tautness at the start of each length.

Continue the tautness achieved from the push-off throughout the entire length. This is harder to do when swimming at 70% effort.

TAUTNESS LEVEL 4 | Workout

Stretch cords

Warm-up: 400 easy swim

WARM-UP/TAUTNESS TECHNICAL

1 × 700 as 100 kick/100 swim continuous with fins

Kick on your back, arms outstretched overhead, thumbs interlaced, palms facing up.

Stationary head position, stable upper body, and three touch points with the surface (head, butt, and tips of fins).

6 × 50 as 25 kick/25 swim with snorkel (no fins) progressive effort with 0:15 rest

Progress effort to 80–85% by the fourth 50, and then hold that effort for the remaining 50s.

Thumbs interlaced and arms fully outstretched, arms by your ears, and palms facing down. Maintain stable torso, no wobbling. Three touch points with the surface: head, butt, heels.

8 × 0:15 vertical kicking with 0:20 rest

Keep your body in a straight line, hips stacked over feet, shoulders over hips, head over shoulders. Fingertips are above the surface of the water, hands in line with shoulders. Maintain upright body position with a small, fast kick, big toes turned slightly inward.

Swim 10:00 at 70% effort with snorkel

Execute the three touch points (back of the head, butt, heels) and excellent body posture.

MAIN SET

6 × 25 swim with snorkel and kickboard (no fins) progressive effort with 0:20 rest

Progress effort until the fourth 25 is fast, and sustain that effort for the remaining 25s.

Three touch points, stable torso, and stationary head.

6 × 25 swim fast on 0:30

Fast swims force proper taut body posture. No equipment.

Access maximum power and propulsion as quickly as possible. Kicking should be narrow, with minimal knee bend, pointed toes, and elevated legs.

1 × 150 at 70% effort with 0:30 rest

Execute perfect wall push-offs to stimulate tautness at the start of each length.

Continue the tautness achieved from the push-off throughout the entire length. This is harder to do when swimming at 70% effort.

ALIGNMENT

After we have mastered the fundamentals of tautness, it is time to move on to alignment. This is where most swimming mistakes occur, and performance suffers as a result. Let's start by identifying what causes alignment problems so we can help eliminate the symptoms: incorrect head movement, rotation, or hand entry. Each of these three problems creates a domino effect that can sabotage your technique and efficiency (see Table 4.1). You must address the real cause of the problem to eliminate the undesirable effects. If you focus on fixing the effects or symptoms of the problems, it's unlikely you will improve your technical alignment. Let's address the primary problems so you feel the benefit that comes with proper alignment.

Head Position

Here's a simple mantra to cue correct head position: no lifting, no tucking, no tilting. Simply rotate your head to the side to breathe. Any other head movement can create misalignment. To achieve this, start with a fixed-head position, in which the tip of your nose is pointing toward the bottom of the pool, and the surface of the water is at approximately mid-head. (Note that this is not to be confused with mid-forehead, which would mean that your head is tipped upward, eyes looking forward.)

TABLE 4.1. CAUSES OF ALIGNMENT PROBLEMS

	Cause	Effect
1	▸ Erroneous or excessive head movement	Excessive rotation, improper body position, body misalignment
2	▸ Excessive shoulder, torso, or hip rotation	Inefficient breathing, slow cadence, widened leg spread
3	▸ Improper hand entry, and hand placement when swimming (beneath the surface)	Fishtailing, shorter, less powerful underwater swim pattern, misdirected body position

Before and after you take a breath, your head position should remain fixed, with as little movement as possible. Water turbulence can affect a stationary or static head position, but try to minimize this until it's time to breathe again.

Head movement can occur in a number of ways:

Lifting: Your chin elevates upward, away from your collarbone.

Tucking: Your chin drops closer to your collarbone.

Tilting: Your head moves off your spine line in a sideways motion.

After you begin to turn your head for a breath, you'll want to minimize the gap, or the space between your head and the shoulder of the extended arm. The gap widens with head tilting, which results in misalignment because the head has moved out of alignment with the spine, which results in a swaying out of the hips.

CORRECT   The head remains fixed, rotating in alignment with the axis of the body.

INCORRECT   Excessive movement of the head, out of alignment with the body axis rather than rotating only, leads to negative consequences: (1) a broken line, (2) a gap between the extended arm and head occurs, creating massive drag, and (3) a misaligned body starts taking shape.

The overrotation of head and hips makes the body "fishtail" as it moves through the water.

Keep the turn of your head and breathing crisp, beginning to inhale as soon as your mouth clears the water. Your mouth returns to the water immediately after taking a breath. Don't linger or "hang out" when taking a breath, or you will cause excessive shoulder, torso, or hip rotation and subsequent breathing problems, which we will take a closer look at now.

Rotation and Breathing

Here we encounter a chicken-or-egg dilemma: Does excessive rotation cause you to linger when breathing—or does the need for adequate oxygen caused by breath lingering result in excessive rotation? Fortunately, it's not that binary. There are schools of swimming and triathlon swimming instruction that promote excessive body rotation as a means for propulsion and bilateral breathing (breathing to both sides) or breathing less frequently than every two strokes. Although these strategies might work for individuals with competitive swim backgrounds, they usually create misalignment for budding triathletes.

Be in the habit of breathing every two strokes or one complete arm cycle. By breathing several times to the right for a specified distance and then switching to the left for the same distance, you can get the benefits of bilateral breathing without sacrificing precious oxygen. It will take some adaptation for many, but it is most definitely a performance enhancer. When it comes to oxygen, frequency is your friend. (We will take a closer look at breathing technique in Chapter 5.)

Ultimately, excessive shoulder, torso, and hip rotation compromise speed in less-advanced swimmers—that is, any swimmer slower than 55 minutes for an Ironman swim, 28 minutes for a 70.3 swim, or 22 minutes for a mile. Excessive rotation slows cadence, which inhibits velocity and may lead to lingering breathing—and this delay generally leads to misalignment. Keep your rotation to less than 45 degrees.

CORRECT Control the rotation of your body to 45 degrees.

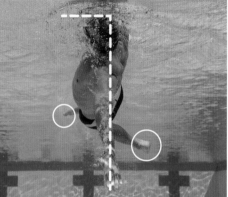

INCORRECT Excessive rotation of the torso throws the entire body out of alignment. See how the kick has splayed and the stroke is compromised.

INCORRECT Overrotation typically causes a swimmer to linger when breathing, which further slows stroke rate and speed.

BILATERAL BREATHING is a worthy skill, but it should not be executed every third stroke. No triathlete should practice extending breathing beyond every two strokes or one arm cycle. Holding your breath or waiting too long to expel air before turning to breathe is highly problematic because oxygen is your greatest energy supplier in an endurance event. This is in stark contrast to the 50- or 100-meter freestyle event at the Olympics. These athletes race for 20 to 55 seconds, so they can ration oxygen for enhanced performance. You should not be doing this in a triathlon, regardless of the distance.

When triathletes with a noncompetitive swim background breathe less frequently than every two strokes, by the time they breathe they tend to gasp, attempting to take in a huge amount of oxygen. This leads to lingering at the surface, which ultimately causes overrotation and various iterations of misalignment. It's important to fix the cause rather than treat the symptom: Breathe more frequently.

Alignment Drills for Controlled Rotation

This set of alignment drills focuses on rotation. Start with a snorkel and fins, and when you feel comfortable holding your body in rotation, incorporate breathing, still using the fins (no snorkel). Kicking on your side without equipment is an advanced kicking technique we discuss in Chapter 6.

Kicking on side with fins and snorkel

Extend your left arm straight out in front of you, palm facing the bottom of the pool. Your hand should be approximately 2–4 inches beneath the water's surface—this is important. Position your other arm at your side, resting comfortably.

Hold your body in a rotated position, about 45–60 degrees at most. Press your jawbone against the inside of your shoulder and point your nose at the bottom of the pool.

Kicking on side with fins, no snorkel

Now remove the snorkel and incorporate breathing. Turn your head to breathe without rotating your torso or hips, keeping your head close to your shoulder (only allowing a very small gap, if any) as it turns to the side for a breath. Immediately after inhalation, return your head back to its fixed position.

Hand Entry and Swim Pattern

It is easiest to think about alignment after we have a good understanding of the imaginary channels we have around us as we swim. With your head aligned with your spine and nose pointed to the bottom of the pool, imagine an axis continuing from your head past your toes; this is the center line. As your right arm enters the water, it should enter directly in front of and in line with your right shoulder; this represents the right line, running parallel to the center axis. As your left arm enters the water, it should enter directly in front of and in line with your left shoulder; this represents the left line. These three lines define the two channels: The right arm stays within the channel between the center line and the right shoulder line; the left arm stays within the channel between the left shoulder line and the center line.

The pulling arm enters the water aligned with the shoulder and remains in its channel, not crossing the midline.

If your hand enters the water outside of this channel or crosses over the center line, misalignment problems will start occurring. For example, if you breathe to the right side and move your head too far to the right, this might cause your left hand to cross over the center line as it enters the water. This then causes your hips and legs to wiggle to the left and come out of alignment—it will be impossible to keep your body in a straight line. This ultimately creates more drag; your body is not cutting the narrowest path through the water, meaning you will swim more slowly and be less efficient. But if we fix your head tilt, which caused this chain of events, your hand can enter the water in line with the shoulder, and the alignment problem will be resolved.

After the hand enters the water and begins the underwater phase, we want to see it move within this imaginary channel between the shoulder line and the center line; it must stay within the boundaries of the channel all the way through to the end of the stroke as the hand exits past the hip. If this has occurred, then good alignment follows.

One of the best ways to practice proper alignment is through pulling. Using a snorkel, empty buoy, and ankle strap, we undertake a variety of pull sets to help

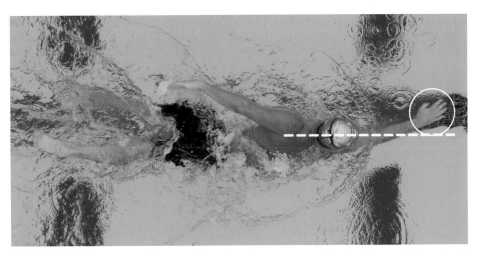

INCORRECT Crossing over the center line on hand entry compromises the alignment of your head, sternum, belly button, and pelvis, knees, and ankles. No fishtailing!

master alignment. The snorkel helps to keep the head still and on the spine line (as the snorkel negates the need to turn the head to breathe), and the buoy and ankle strap help secure the hips, legs, and feet. It is a perfect opportunity to really get a sense of what proper alignment feels like. You can also easily start to feel it as soon as you come out of alignment: No fishtailing allowed!

After the pull set is complete, take the pulling gear off and try to mimic that same alignment as you swim. To begin with, it might be possible to hold it for a few laps, but then it starts to break down. With consistent practice over a sustained period, you will see improvement.

The **"S" PULL** is a technique taught by the late US Olympic swim coach James "Doc" Counsilman. It involves pulling and pushing water with an outsweep, an insweep, and a finishing outsweep. There is merit (and spirited debate around) this teaching for certain types of swimmers, namely those with advanced skills and experience. Most triathletes will be better served by generating a simple directional force to pull and then push the water straight backward without attempting outsweeps or insweeps.

4-Step Drill Progression to Achieve Alignment in Hand Channels

Step 1: One-arm drill with snorkel and fins

Extend one arm out in front of you, in line with your shoulder. Hold the opposite arm stationary again in line with your shoulder. Your palm will face downward, about 2–4 inches below the water's surface.

Start pulling with your swimming arm, staying within the channel between the center line and the shoulder line. At the completion of a stroke cycle, as the hand reenters the water, it will never touch the extended hand; in fact, it is placed directly in front of its shoulder, creating parallel-looking arms.

Step 2: One-arm drill with fins, no snorkel

Remove the snorkel and repeat the drill, keeping the pulling arm within its channel. Control your rotation as you breathe, short and crisp.

Step 3: One-arm drill with snorkel, no fins

Using just a snorkel and no fins, focus on keeping your body taut and pulling with good alignment.

Step 4: One-arm drill without equipment

After practicing the first three steps, repeat the drill without equipment. Keep the pulling arm moving efficiently and smoothly.

Pulling with ankle strap, snorkel, and empty buoy

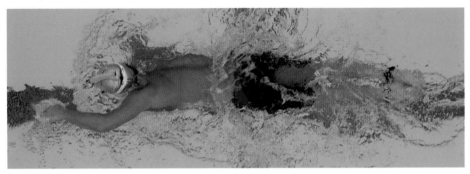

Hold your body with the appropriate muscle tension and tautness. Engage the muscles in your lower back, hamstrings, and core to aid in holding your legs closer to the surface.

When using the ankle strap, body alignment becomes even more critical: head, chest, belly button, and the center of your hips, knees, ankles, and feet need to remain aligned. Point your toes and turn them slightly inward, thus having big toes touching or almost touching. This helps your legs be fairly taut, removing any bend in the knees. Keep your head absolutely stationary. The tip of your nose points to the bottom of the pool, perpendicular to the water's surface.

Pulling with ankle strap, snorkel, and buoy with chambers filled

With the extra buoy weight, you'll need a faster cadence. This negates any glide after the hand enters the water. Extend your hand forward and downward to start the propulsive phase sooner. More force is applied through the hand and forearm as tension in the wrist remains firm during the propulsive phase. Keep your fingertips pointed toward the bottom of the pool during the propulsive phase.

Mastering this drill requires muscular tension as one arm executes the power phase while simultaneously relaxing muscular tension in the recovering arm (from the point where the hand exits the water to re-entry). This drill must

be executed with the appropriate dosage of effort to stabilize muscles so that the legs remain as close to the water's surface as possible while keeping your body aligned—it's a monumental task. Be patient!

PROPER ALIGNMENT | Keys

- ▸ Your body is in a straight line from your head to your toes, and you can maintain that alignment as you swim. Your head remains aligned with your spine through all phases of the stroke.
- ▸ Your body is perpendicular to the pool walls and/or parallel to the side walls of the pool (providing the pool is rectangular).
- ▸ Your arms and legs remain in their respective channels. Your hand enters the water *directly* in line with your right shoulder. As you extend it forward, keep it in alignment with your shoulder line. Do not let your arm cross the center line or sweep too far outward at any point.
- ▸ Keep your fingertips pointed downward as you pull. Each hand executes long, smooth, efficient swim strokes within that narrow channel.

Distance per stroke (DPS) is a measure of stroke efficiency and is designed to take the stroke count as low as possible per length in order to cover the most distance per arm stroke. With DPS it is easy to get caught up in trying to take as few strokes as possible, overlooking the fact that this might not necessarily lead to faster or better swimming. For example, I would estimate that at the peak of his fitness, Michael Phelps could swim across a 25-yard/meter pool in six or seven strokes, which, of course, highlights his incredible efficiency, but he would never have dreamt of racing with that low of a stroke count. In general, we must not prioritize efficiency ahead of speed or stroke rate because it can lead to slower swimming, especially in open water. Remember that DPS (or stroke efficiency) is not the only factor that will help us swim faster. Performance is a product of efficiency and stroke rate (how fast we can turn our arms over). For triathletes, I recommend a slightly higher focus on stroke rate in pool workouts and a much higher focus on stroke rate when racing or training in open water.

Experienced swimmers who achieve great DPS (that is, cover a considerable distance with each arm stroke) can typically generate a huge amount of propulsion per arm stroke. Their powerful underwater propulsion can often make their swimming look swan-like, as if they were gliding across the pool with seemingly little effort. These long, smooth strokes—almost catch-up-style swimming—look elegant, and it is not surprising that mere mortals want to emulate them, and inexperienced coaches promote the style at a high cost. But do not be fooled: Although all you can see above the surface is their effortless arm recovery, beneath the water there is some serious force being generated. These are elite swimmers who can clock less than 50 seconds for a 100-yard/meter swim while holding stroke rates in excess of 80 strokes per minute. That kind of swimming does not come without significant power and propulsion under the water and years of training. The average age-group triathlete does not have the luxury of this kind of propulsion. And further slowing down stroke rate in an attempt to achieve the seductive DPS leads to a great deal of deceleration, especially when swimming in open water, the opposite of what we are hoping to achieve. In my experience, triathletes focusing too greatly on DPS might make their stroke look pretty and even gain some efficiency, but these come at the cost of speed and performance. You need both: DPS and cadence.

ALIGNMENT LEVEL 1 | Workout

Stretch cords

Warm-up: 10:00 easy swim

WARM-UP/TAUTNESS AND ALIGNMENT

8 × 100 as 50 kick/50 swim with snorkel, fins, and kickboard, with 0:20 rest

Progress effort every two intervals.

Stabilize your torso when kicking and focus on the three touch points with the water's surface.

1 × 400 swim with snorkel and fins at 70% effort

Keep your head still and your nose pointed toward the bottom of the pool: no lifting, turning, or tucking the chin.

DRILL SET

Do 2 rounds of this set, focusing on head position while breathing.

1 × 200 kicking on side with fins at 70% effort with 0:30 rest

Hold 45-degree (not 90-degree) rotation, with bottom arm outstretched, palm facing the bottom of the pool. Press your ear against the outstretched arm (no gap!), and press your other arm against your side. Point your nose at the bottom of the pool, and when you turn to breathe, maintain the same distance between your ear and your arm. Don't tuck, tilt, or lift your head.

4 × 25 kicking on side with fins, at 80% effort with 0:30 rest

Keep your torso and hips stable when turning your head to breathe.

4 × 50 swim with fins at 80–85% effort with 0:15 rest

MAIN SET

1 × 800 pull with empty pull buoy and ankle strap (no snorkel) at 70% effort with 0:45 rest

Aim for excellent alignment and a crisp head turn for a quick breath.

8 × 100 swim at 80% effort with 0:20 rest

Maintain tautness, excellent push-offs, and crisp breaths with no lifting, tilting, or tucking of the chin.

Rest 1:00

8 × 50 swim at 85% effort with 0:15 rest

Increase effort for additional stress while still focusing on all of your technical elements.

ALIGNMENT LEVEL 2 | Workout

Stretch cords

Warm-up: 10:00 easy swim

WARM-UP/TAUTNESS AND ALIGNMENT

8 × 100 as 50 kick/50 swim with snorkel, fins, and kickboard, with 0:20 rest

Progress effort every two intervals.

Stabilize your torso when kicking and focus on the three touch points with the water's surface, nose pointed toward the bottom of the pool; no lifting, turning, or tucking the chin.

1 × 400 swim with snorkel and fins at 70% effort

Keep your head still and your nose pointed toward the bottom of the pool; no lifting, turning, or tucking the chin.

DRILL SET

Do 2 rounds of this set, focusing on head position while breathing.

1 × 200 kicking on side with fins at 70% effort with 0:30 rest

Hold 45-degree (not 90-degree) rotation, with bottom arm outstretched, palm facing the bottom of the pool. Press your cheek against the outstretched arm (no gap!), and press your other arm against your side. Point your nose at the bottom of the pool, and when you turn to breathe, maintain the same distance between your head and your arm. Don't tuck, tilt, or lift your head.

4 × 25 kicking on side with fins, at 80% effort with 0:30 rest

Keep your torso and hips stable when turning your head to breathe.

4 × 50 swim with fins at 80–85% effort with 0:15 rest

MAIN SET

1 × 700 pull with empty pull buoy and ankle strap (no snorkel) at 70% effort with 0:45 rest

Aim for excellent alignment and a crisp head turn for a quick breath.

7 × 100 swim at 80% effort with 0:20 rest

Maintain tautness, excellent push-offs, and crisp breaths with no lifting, tilting, or tucking of the chin.

Rest 1:00

7 × 50 swim at 85% effort with 0:15 rest

Increase effort for additional stress while still focusing on all of your technical elements.

ALIGNMENT LEVEL 3 | Workout

Stretch cords

Warm-up: 10:00 easy swim

WARM-UP/TAUTNESS AND ALIGNMENT

8 × 100 as 50 kick/50 swim with snorkel, fins, and kickboard, with 0:20 rest

Progress effort every two intervals.

Stabilize your torso when kicking, and focus on the three touch points with the water's surface, nose pointed toward the bottom of the pool; no lifting, turning, or tucking the chin.

1 × 350 swim with snorkel and fins at 70% effort

Keep your head still and your nose pointed toward the bottom of the pool; no lifting, turning, or tucking the chin.

DRILL SET

Do 2 rounds of this set, focusing on head position while breathing.

1 × 200 kicking on side with fins at 70% effort with 0:30 rest

Hold 45-degree (not 90-degree) rotation, with bottom arm outstretched, palm facing the bottom of the pool. Press your ear against the outstretched arm (no gap!), and press your other arm against your side. Point your nose at the bottom of the pool, and when you turn to breathe, maintain the same distance between your ear and your arm. Don't tuck, tilt, or lift your head.

4 × 25 kicking on side with fins, at 80% effort with 0:30 rest

Keep your torso and hips stable when turning your head to breathe.

3 × 50 swim with fins at 80–85% effort with 0:15 rest

MAIN SET

1 × 600 pull with empty pull buoy and ankle strap (no snorkel) at 70% effort with 0:45 rest

Aim for excellent alignment and a crisp head turn for a quick breath.

7 × 100 swim at 80% effort with 0:20 rest

Maintain tautness, excellent push-offs, and crisp breaths with no lifting, tilting, or tucking of the chin.

Rest 1:00

7 × 50 swim at 85% effort with 0:15 rest

Increase effort for additional stress while still focusing on all of your technical elements.

ALIGNMENT LEVEL 4 | Workout

Stretch cords

Warm-up: 10:00 easy swim

WARM-UP/TAUTNESS AND ALIGNMENT

8 × 100 as 50 kick/50 swim with snorkel, fins, and kickboard

Progress effort every 2 repeats, taking 0:20 rest between each.

Stabilize your torso when kicking, and focus on the three touch points with the water's surface (back of head, butt, heels).

1 × 300 swim with snorkel and fins at 70% effort

Focus on keeping your head still with your nose pointed toward the bottom of the pool; no lifting, turning, or tucking the chin.

DRILL SET

Do 2 rounds of this set, focusing on hand position when breathing.

1 × 200 kicking on your side with fins at 70% effort with 0:30 rest

Hold 45-degree (not 90-degree) rotation, with bottom arm outstretched, palm facing the bottom of the pool. Press your ear against the outstretched arm (no gap!), and press your other arm against your side. Point your nose at the bottom of the pool, and when you turn to breathe, maintain the same distance between your ear and your arm. Don't tuck, tilt, or lift your head.

4 × 25 kicking on side with fins at 80% effort with 0:30 rest

Keep your torso and hips stable when turning your head to breathe.

3 × 50 swim with fins at 80–85% effort with 0:15 rest

MAIN SET

1 × 500 pull with empty pull buoy and ankle strap (no snorkel) at 70% effort with 0:45 rest

Aim for excellent alignment and a crisp head turn for a quick breath.

5 × 100 swim at 80% effort with 0:20 rest

Maintain tautness, excellent push-offs, and crisp breaths with no lifting, tilting, or tucking of the chin.

Rest 1:00.

5 × 50 swim at 85% effort with 0:15 rest

Increase effort for additional stress while still focusing on all of your technical elements.

PROPULSION

Propulsion is most easily understood through two phases: the set-up phase and the power phase. Watching a fast swimmer move across the pool with grace and seemingly little effort can be beguiling and even frustrating for a novice. "How do they do that?" The answer: "Propulsion." But don't jump the gun—this is the final step in the progression of skills and education. It can be tackled only after tautness and alignment are acquired.

If athletes are swimming 60 strokes per minute, that is, a single arm stroke per second, thus 60 total single-arm strokes in 60 seconds, they are performing on average 1 stroke per second, which is no time at all, but it is critical that each element is executed correctly.

Set-Up Phase

This is most commonly referred to as the "catch." The hand enters the water in the channel between the center line and the shoulder line, at almost full extension. The hand then extends forward and downward, never upward. During this conclusion of the set-up, the fingers are ideally pointing downward toward the bottom of the pool, without any bending of the wrist. Simultaneously, the arm goes from being nearly straight to having a slight bend at the elbow, creating a 100–120-degree angle. The elbow then moves so it is pointed toward the side wall. It remains positioned above the wrist throughout the stroke, never dropping beneath it or pointing toward the bottom of the pool. When executed well, the set-up phase puts you in position for the second phase of propulsion, the power phase.

The set-up phase of the stroke starts with the arm extending forward and downward, never upward.

Set-up is complete when the fingertips are pointed toward the bottom of the pool.

Propulsion Drills for the Set-up Phase

Set-up drill with buoy and snorkel

Using a snorkel and buoy, float with both arms extended in front of you, hands in front of the shoulders like straight railroad tracks; the hands should never be touching each other. You stay in place and are simply practicing the initial movement of setting up the stroke for its propulsive phase. This should be a slow downward movement of the arm and hand so that your hand goes from being parallel with the bottom of the pool to being perpendicular to it. There should be no forward body movement; you are simply moving your hand and rehearsing that initial, nonpropulsive stroke set-up. As your arms move downward, your elbows start bending at approximately 120 degrees, staying above the wrist and hand, while pointing to the pool's side walls.

Pause for 1–2 seconds and recover your arm back to the surface, underwater. Pause again for 1–2 seconds and repeat.

Arms fully extended, palms facing downward, 2–4 inches beneath the surface, eyes facing downward.

Set-up: At conclusion, fingertips pointed downward, straight line from elbow to fingertips, elbows bent and pointed to the side walls.

After pausing from the set-up, hands then recover forward.

Hands continue recovering forward toward full extension.

Shown here without the snorkel, as your arms move downward, your elbows start bending at approximately 120 degrees, staying above the wrist and hand, while pointing to the pool's side walls. How close your elbow is to the water's surface depends on your flexibility and mobility. A slightly deeper elbow is encouraged for triathletes.

Power Phase

Both hand and wrist tension and directional force are necessary in the power phase. Without adequate tension, the hand and wrist will not be able to "grab" the water and hold on to it, which compromises the ability to generate adequate propulsion. When a swimmer fails to move water with both force and speed, I call this "petting the kitty": attempting to move water with the gentle touch one might use to stroke a cat. This won't work!

After you are able to hold the water with adequate hand and wrist tension, directional force comes into play. The hand drives backward, toward the hip, always staying within its channel, between the center line and the shoulder line, beneath the body. This hand drive does not happen at a consistent speed: Propulsion requires acceleration. The hand should accelerate to ballistic pace through the water as it pushes back. Use force to hold on to the water as you set up, then pull and push it. There can be no softness here! We want to see a firm, powerful force applied to the water. Throughout the power phase, the elbow remains elevated above the wrist.

In short, perhaps the best way to think of the two phases of propulsion is simply "grip it and rip it," that is, implement the set-up (grip it), and accelerate the hand through the water (rip it). Recover your arm, and the process begins again.

Propulsion improves as your connectivity improves. We want to see connection between your hand movement and rotation of your body. As your hand is pulling and pushing through the water, it needs to coordinate with the rotation of your hips and shoulders. Practice and consistency are key to establishing this advanced skill.

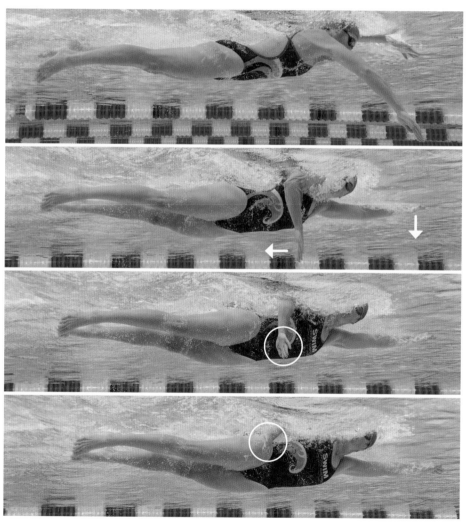

Propulsion happens in the power phase as the hand grips the water in the set-up phase and then accelerates, pushing the water backward. Note the position of the hand and wrist through the stroke cycle—the fingers are always pointed downward.

Propulsion drill with buoy and snorkel

Post stroke set-up, do the following: Start with your fingertips pointed toward the bottom of the pool, keeping your wrist and hand firm and flat at 180 degrees.

Begin executing the power and propulsive phase. Pull and then push your hands backward, keeping fingertips pointed straight down. Maintain adequate tension in the wrist and hand through the pull phase. As you transition to the push phase—toward the end of the stroke, near your midsection—the hand to wrist angle will change to be a wider, obtuse angle.

Pulling with ankle strap, snorkel, buoy, and tech paddles

Wrap your hands firmly around the paddle's spindle, keeping your fingers in contact with the spindle.

As the propulsive phase begins, make sure your knuckles are pointed at the bottom of the pool. The shape and structure of the paddles reinforce proper wrist position *by not allowing* hand flexion—any angle less than 180 degrees between hand and forearm, which happens when the wrist is angled downward.

Pull sets without a buoy achieve three important objectives:

1. Force the required body tautness; otherwise legs sink.
2. Demand proper alignment; otherwise body wiggles out of alignment.
3. Necessitate adequate hand tension for propulsion; otherwise performance suffers.

Focal points are all about these three properties: tautness, alignment, and propulsion. This is an advanced drill.

Pulling with an ankle strap and snorkel (no buoy)

Push off the wall powerfully. This sets up tautness. Pull at a higher effort to maintain a taut posture. A higher cadence rate also facilitates taut posture, but more importantly, it helps your legs remain closer to the water's surface.

Perpetual arm and hand movement is essential. Eliminate any type of catch-up swimming-style swimming as this creates propulsive dead spots or massive velocity retardation.

Engage your core, lower back, and hamstrings to assist in keeping your legs toward the surface. If your legs are sinking, do 1–2 butterfly kicks every 25 yards/meters to help return the legs to the surface.

Early vertical forearm (EVF) refers to the beginning of the pull when swimming freestyle. It involves immediately keeping the elbow high, near the surface of the water, as the pull phase is being set up for propulsion. EVF gained popularity after underwater footage captured Australian swim superstars Ian Thorpe and Grant Hackett using this technique. More recently, EVF has seeped into the triathlon swimming space. It's my opinion that this technique is hugely overrated and almost impossible for most triathletes to physically achieve.

There are considerable differences between the flexibility and mobility of elite swimmers and age-group triathletes. Swimmers are incredibly limber, especially in their upper bodies, gained from years of flexibility training, and this affords some of them the ability to swim with EVF. When the hand enters the water, the elbow moves up to the surface of the water almost immediately to start executing the power phase. When most triathletes attempt this, it often causes other errors in their stroke mechanics. Triathletes typically lack the flexibility of younger swimmers, in part because of aging, the corrosive effect that cycling and running can have on the body's mobility, and the lack of an elite swimmer's years of flexibility practice. Expecting a triathlete to execute a movement in the water that requires such a tremendous amount of mobility is a big ask. I have seen former swimmers-turned-triathletes attempting to do this and struggling, which has left me believing that it is simply something that should not be forced. To be clear: We always want to see the elbow above the wrist, but this does not need to happen as early in the pull phase. It's perfectly fine for the elbow to be a foot or more below the water's surface as it begins the pull phase. This significantly lessens the load on the shoulder and does not require an incredible amount of flexibility or mobility.

Of course, many people see elite swimmers doing something like EVF and try to mimic them, forgetting the pedigree of these athletes and the many thousands of miles they have swum in their lifetimes. EVF is not without its benefits—but I cannot begin to agree with those who believe it is *the* single-most important key to faster swimming. I am a huge fan of learning new things and understanding new concepts, but to me the merits of EVF fall well short, like some new supplement with all its hype.

There are plenty of decorated elite swimmers who show no evidence of EVF. Their elbows always remain above their wrists as they set up their stroke and pull the water, but they swim with a deeper arm stroke, which to me seems more profitable, especially

Early vertical forearm is not recommended for triathletes. In the first photo you can see an *early* vertical forearm—the arm is more shallow and the elbow is closer to the surface. In the second photo the arm is deeper and distance between the elbow and the surface is greater.

for triathletes. Of course, if EVF is something that works for you, then continue to do it, but do not blindly chase it as a solution to your swimming ailments. In my view, it is not the best way for the majority of triathletes to swim. Drop your arm slightly deeper and engage your lats, which are bigger, more powerful muscles.

ACHIEVING PROPULSION | Keys

- ▶ Enter your hand into the water, a few inches from full extension.
- ▶ Place your hand out in front of you, anywhere between your shoulder and head.
- ▶ Simultaneously extend your hand forward and downward.
- ▶ Keep a straight line from palm to forearm, with no bending at the wrist.
- ▶ Extend your arm downward so that your elbow bends and pops up, pointing to the side walls (a vertical forearm, but not an early vertical forearm).
- ▶ Grab on to the water with forearm and palm, fingertips pointed at the bottom of the pool. This is the "grip it" segment.
- ▶ Now rip it! After gripping the water, rip it backward while keeping a firm wrist. No loose wrists here please; it's all about holding firm tension—and keeping your fingers pointed to the bottom.
- ▶ Push the water all the way back, creating the longest possible pull, until the hand exits at the hip to begin the arm recovery.

PROPULSION LEVEL 1 | Workout

Stretch cords

Warm-up: 500 easy swim

WARM-UP/TAUTNESS

1 × 1000 kick/swim with snorkel, fins, and kickboard, gently progressing effort over continuous swim set: 200 kick, 200 swim, 150 kick, 150 swim, 100 kick, 100 swim, 50 kick, 50 swim

Keep your head fixed and torso stabilized.

WARM-UP/ALIGNMENT

6 × 100 kick with fins as 50 kicking on side/50 swim, progressive effort, with 0:20 rest

With kicking drill, focus on having no gaps between your head and cheek and crisp head turns to take a breath.

SKILL WORK ALIGNMENT IN HAND CHANNELS

4 × 100 with fins at 70% effort with 0:20 rest

1. Right arm only
2. Left arm only
3. Alternate single-arm work every 3 strokes
4. Regular swim

4 × 100 at 70% effort with no equipment, same pattern as previous set

MAIN SET

1 × 400 with snorkel at 70% effort with 0:40 rest

Set-up: On entry, see that your arm is bent at approximately 120 degrees, with your fingertips pointing toward the bottom of the pool. Keep your elbow elevated higher than your wrist, away from your sides, and pointed toward the wall of the pool. With the snorkel on, you can visually check the position of your arm as you swim.

6 × 100 swim at 80% effort with 0:20 rest

Start at 70% effort and progress to 80% by the third set. Sustain effort for the remaining swims.

Set-up: On entry, extend your hand in a forward and downward motion, moving to an elevated elbow position (higher than your wrist) and positioning your fingers toward the bottom of the pool.

Stretch cords

Warm-up: 450 easy swim

WARM-UP/TAUTNESS

1 × 1000 kick/swim with snorkel, fins, and kickboard, gently progressing effort over continuous swim set: 200 kick, 200 swim, 150 kick, 150 swim, 100 kick, 100 swim, 50 kick, 50 swim

Keep your head fixed and torso stabilized.

WARM-UP/ALIGNMENT

6 × 100 kick with fins as 50 kicking on side/50 swim, progressive effort, with 0:20 rest

With kicking drill, focus on having no gaps between your head and cheek and crisp head turns to take a breath.

SKILL WORK ALIGNMENT IN HAND CHANNELS

4 × 100 kick with fins at 70% effort with 0:20 rest

1. Right arm only
2. Left arm only
3. Alternate single-arm work every 3 strokes
4. Regular swim

4 × 100 at 70% effort with no equipment, same pattern as previous set

MAIN SET

1 × 350 with snorkel at 70% effort with 0:40 rest

Set-up: On entry, see that your arm is bent at approximately 120 degrees, with your fingertips pointing toward the bottom of the pool. Keep your elbow elevated higher than your wrist, away from your sides, and pointed toward the wall of the pool. With the snorkel on, you can visually check the position of your arm as you swim.

5 × 100 swim at 80% effort with 0:20 rest

Start at 70% effort and progress to 80% by the third set. Sustain effort for the remaining swims.

Set-up: On entry, extend your hand in a forward and downward motion, moving to an elevated elbow position (higher than your wrist), and positioning your fingers toward the bottom of the pool.

PROPULSION LEVEL 3 | Workout

Stretch cords

Warm-up: 400 easy swim

WARM-UP/TAUTNESS

1 × 1000 kick/swim with snorkel, fins, and kickboard, gently progressing effort over continuous swim set: 200 kick, 200 swim, 150 kick, 150 swim, 100 kick, 100 swim, 50 kick, 50 swim

Keep your head fixed and torso stabilized.

WARM-UP/ALIGNMENT

6 × 100 kick with fins as 50 kicking on side/50 swim, progressive effort, with 0:20 rest

With kicking drill, focus on having no gaps between your head and cheek and crisp head turns to take a breath.

SKILL WORK ALIGNMENT IN HAND CHANNELS

4 × 75 with fins at 70% effort with 0:20 rest

1. Right arm only
2. Left arm only
3. Alternate single-arm work every 3 strokes
4. Regular swim

4 × 75 at 70% effort with no equipment, same pattern as previous set

MAIN SET

1 × 300 with snorkel at 70% effort with 0:40 rest

Set-up: On entry, see that your arm is bent at approximately 120 degrees, with your fingertips pointing toward the bottom of the pool. Keep your elbow elevated higher than your wrist, away from your sides, and pointed toward the wall of the pool. With the snorkel on, you can visually check the position of your arm as you swim.

6 × 75 swim at 80% effort with 0:20 rest

Start at 70% effort and progress to 80% by the third set. Sustain effort for the remaining swims.

Set-up: On entry, extend your hand in a forward and downward motion, moving to an elevated elbow position (higher than your wrist), and positioning your fingers toward the bottom of the pool.

PROPULSION LEVEL 4 | Workout

Stretch cords

Warm-up: 350 easy swim

WARM-UP/TAUTNESS

1 × 1000 kick/swim with snorkel, fins, and kickboard, gently progressing effort over continuous swim set: 200 kick, 200 swim, 150 kick, 150 swim, 100 kick, 100 swim, 50 kick, 50 swim

Keep your head fixed and torso stabilized.

WARM-UP/ALIGNMENT

5 × 100 kick with fins as 50 kicking on side/50 swim, progressive effort, with 0:20 rest

With kicking drill, focus on having no gaps between your head and cheek and crisp head turns to take a breath.

SKILL WORK ALIGNMENT IN HAND CHANNELS

4 × 75 with fins at 70% effort with 0:20 rest

1. Right arm only
2. Left arm only
3. Alternate single-arm work every 3 strokes
4. Regular swim

4 × 75 at 70% effort with no equipment, same pattern as previous set

MAIN SET

1 × 250 swim with snorkel at 70% effort with 0:40 rest

Set-up: On entry, see that your arm is bent at approximately 120 degrees, with your fingertips pointing toward the bottom of the pool. Keep your elbow elevated higher than your wrist, away from your sides, and pointed toward the wall of the pool. With the snorkel on, you can visually check the position of your arm as you swim.

5 × 75 swim at 80% effort with 0:20 rest

Start at 70% effort and progress to 80% by the third set. Sustain effort for the remaining swims.

Set-up: On entry, extend your hand in a forward and downward motion, moving to an elevated elbow position (higher than your wrist), and positioning your fingers toward the bottom of the pool.

TECHNIQUE CAPSTONE | Workout

Stretch cords

Warm-up: 5:00–10:00 easy swim

TAUTNESS FOCUS

8 × 100 as 50 kick/50 swim with fins and snorkel at 70–75% effort with 0:20 rest

Keep a long, taut frame.

1 × 5:00 swim using fins and snorkel at 70% effort

Focus on holding head position fixed and your three touch points (back of the head, butt, and heels) at the surface of the water.

5 × 0:30 vertical kicking with 0:20 rest

ALIGNMENT FOCUS

6 × 100 as 2 rounds of 3 × 100, 50 drill/50 swim with 0:20 rest

1. Left arm extended, swimming with your right arm only for 50, then 50 full-stroke swim
2. Right arm extended, swimming with your left arm only for 50, then 50 full-stroke swim
3. 3 right-arm strokes, 3 left-arm strokes for 50, then 50 full-stroke swim

Keep the swimming hand within its alignment boundaries.

Progress this drill over the course of two to three weeks in the following order: (1) snorkel and fins, (2) just fins, (3) snorkel only, and (4) without equipment.

PROPULSION FOCUS

4 × 50 swim with snorkel and buoy, with 0:20 rest

Before each 50 swim, do 5 propulsion set-up drills:

Keep a straight line maintained from fingertips to elbow. There is no wrist flexion in the stroke's set-up. After one repetition, stop, pause, and then recover your hand beneath the surface to the starting point to do it again. After 5 of these exercises, immediately swim 50, rest, and repeat.

1 × 5:00 swim with snorkel and buoy at 70% effort, with a dedicated focus on setting up the catch.

HAND TENSION AND FOLLOW-THROUGH DRILL

4 × 25 snorkel and buoy with 0:15 rest

Execute the set-up and pause a second upon completion. Keep a firm hand and wrist as you prepare to grip it and rip it!

Pull and then push the hand backward. Keep fingertips pointed toward the bottom of the pool. Maintain firm tension in the wrist and hand. Maintain the 180-degree, hand-to-wrist angle through the pull phase. While transitioning to the push portion, toward the end of the stroke (around the belly button area), the hand-to-wrist angle changes to a wider angle.

1 × 5:00 swim continuous distance at 70% effort, using both buoy and snorkel

Incorporate the drill elements into full swimming.

SESSION WRAP-UP

8 × 25 at 90% effort with 0:15–0:20 rest. No equipment.

The goal is full-stroke swimming, incorporating all of the technical elements we have been practicing but at faster speeds. Swimming fast forces you to hold the right amount of tension in your body. It also helps you learn to accelerate the hand and apply greater force through the water. The wrist can bend more easily than you think, so be mindful of this and keep it firm.

1 × 5:00 swim at 70% effort. No equipment.

Maintain the elements of proper tautness and propulsion when swimming at a lower effort. It is much more difficult, thus requiring laser focus, especially at the end of the session.

This is our most technically dense session, which comes toward the end of our recovery and technical phase. It is introduced after approximately eight weeks of practicing the various outlined drills, in sequence, for technical development. It is not a session to be done without that foundation or its methodical buildup.

Swim stroke mechanics are complex, but focusing on that complexity does little to help you absorb the knowledge and actually execute the stroke. My goal here is to keep things simple, which is key to learning, understanding, engaging, and executing. Furthermore, the triathlete must always remember that swimming for triathlon is different from other swimming disciplines: Your needs are nuanced, your race demands are precise, and your time is limited. Applying swimming's general brush to all is not always prudent or optimal. And you are, first and foremost, a triathlete.

5

Breathing

BREATHING IS ONE OF THE MOST IMPORTANT and fundamental aspects of good swimming, yet it is also the topic that leads to the most confusion, questions, and misinformation. Plenty of myths abound relating to breathing frequency, rhythm, and timing. The rules relating to breathing for a competitive pool swimmer are entirely different from those for triathlon swimming, and this is especially true when it comes to open-water swimming. If your educational and instructional source does not, cannot, or will not speak to this distinction, get another source.

When it comes to breathing, most athletes have a preferred side to which they breathe: the right or left. If we are referring to breathing every two strokes, then this is simply the turning of the head once per arm cycle. Bilateral breathing refers to breathing on alternating sides, whether that is every three, five, or even seven strokes. For example, the swimmer takes three arm strokes, then breathes to the left, and after another three arm strokes breathes to the right.

It is not uncommon for novice athletes to try to work on holding each breath as long as possible, as if it's some kind of badge of honor. They take one huge breath and try to make it last for five or six strokes before gulping for air and trying to repeat the pattern. By the time they reach the end of the pool, they are exhausted.

Short, crisp, frequent breathing is critical to the demands of triathlon swimming. As you turn your head to breathe, finish expelling air in preparation for the next breath.

Although it's true that competitive pool swimmers can be seen breathing more infrequently, let's remember that 85 percent of competitive swim races are less than two minutes in duration.

Oxygen is an athlete's best friend; it fuels your muscles. It dictates your aerobic capacity and is critical for energy production. You would never consider holding your breath and starving yourself of oxygen while cycling or running, so why do the same when swimming? Elite cyclists and runners take 40 to 50 breaths a minute. If average triathletes are swimming with a stroke rate of 50 to 60 strokes per minute and breathing every third stroke, they are taking 20 breaths (or fewer) a minute. That means they are getting half as much oxygen at best. Now consider that an Ironman swim will require an hour or more for most age-groupers—it's easy to see that this type of oxygen debt is incredibly counterproductive at the outset of such a long endurance event.

I am not contesting the value of bilateral breathing, which helps establish balance. If you only ever breathe to your right side, you might well develop asymmetries in your body. In addition, in open water, your ability to breathe to the left and right allows you to see and be aware of what is happening on either side of you and manage conditions. For this reason, I advise athletes to breathe every two strokes, alternating sides after three or four arm cycles. This pattern of frequency allows for optimal oxygen uptake. It is not uncommon to see front-pack swimmers breathing to their left side for three or four arm cycles, then breathing to their right for the next three or four arm cycles. They keep repeating this pattern throughout their entire race, ensuring both optimal oxygen intake and maximum awareness of what is happening around them.

The goal is to keep your breathing rhythmic, frequent, crisp, and short. Learning to breathe while maintaining good mechanics and efficiency can take time. Start by taking more shallow breaths, which helps you stay in alignment. Efforts to take in a big, deep breaths when swimming typically create all kinds of problems not easy to fix: your head overrotates, your hips sink or move excessively, and your kick spreads wide to try to restore balance. If you focus on calm, frequent breathing, you can avoid these problems altogether. It all starts with one golden rule: Never hold your breath.

If you are a right-sided breather, proper breathing fits in with the natural rhythm of your stroke cycle as follows:

1. As your right hand is at your hip, exiting the water, turn your head to begin taking a breath.
2. Take a short, crisp breath as your arm exits the water and begins its recovery

back to the front to reenter the water. Sharp timing allows your head to begin returning to the water as your right arm finishes its external revolution.

3. Your right arm reenters the water, and your hand sets up for the next propulsive phase. As your right arm moves underwater through the propulsion phase, you are expelling air. Your hand prepares to exit the water again as your head turns to take another breath, and the entire process repeats.

With practice, your breathing will become rhythmic and habitual. Because we only have a short opportunity to take a breath when swimming, it is important to work your breathing into the natural rhythm of your stroke cycle. When you swim, approximately two-thirds of your time is spent with your face submerged.

Inhalation should begin as soon as your mouth clears the water. Your mouth returns to the water immediately after inhalation, with your face down and head fixed, no movement. There is no lingering or additional time spent before or after inhaling with your head to the side; this is absolutely critical. Lingering or hanging out when your head is turned to the side can be caused by overrotation, infrequent breathing (i.e., more than a breath every two arm strokes), or holding your breath. There is no room for breath-holding in triathlon or endurance swimming.

EFFECTIVE BREATHING | Keys

▶ Slowly and gently exhale through your mouth whenever your head is in the water. It is also possible to exhale through the nose, but at more elevated heart rates it is easier to consistently breathe through your mouth.
▶ Turn your head to inhale, in sync with the rotation of your body. For pool swimming, this is a subtle turn of the head, exposing just one goggle above the surface of the water, not your entire face. In dynamic open-water conditions, simply make sure your mouth clears the surface of the water without you lifting or tilting your head.
▶ Keep breaths crisp and shallow, rhythmic and short, without huge gulps or excessive movement. As your torso rotates, move your head to breathe, then inhale, move your head back into the water, and begin the gradual exhale.

OPTIMAL HEAD POSITION

Except when turning to breathe, your head should remain still in the water. Many people tend to move their head after breathing, which can lead to issues elsewhere with body position and alignment. Eliminate extra head movement, and many of these problems are instantly resolved. Using a front-mounted snorkel eliminates the need to think about moving your head to breathe and allows you to focus on a stationary head position. It also helps you keep good body position and alignment.

Traditional swimming wisdom dictates it is best to keep the water line at the top of your forehead so your eyes are looking diagonally ahead at the bottom of the pool. This head position has some value for racing shorter distances, but for triathlon swimming we want to see the tip of your nose pointing to the bottom of the pool and the water line toward the center of the top of your head. If you were watching an athlete swim toward you, you would be able to see the top half of the head; the remaining half is in the water.

HEAD POSITION TEST | Protocol

Draw a black dot on the top of your cap (preferably a light-colored cap) about 3 inches in diameter. Have someone stand at the end of the lane and take a video as you swim toward them. You do not want to see that dot moving up, down, or laterally—we call it the dancing dot. If it is, then you have too much head movement. If it is stationary, then we are witnessing optimal head position in the water. If you're in need of more focused head position work, start with the Alignment Drills in Chapter 4. Head position can be the panacea to so many problems swimmers encounter with their technique. Follow this simple mantra: no lifting, no tucking, no tilting, keep it neutral.

HEAD AND BODY ROTATION

When you are swimming, think of your head and body as one unit: Do not allow them to move independently of each other. If you breathe on the right side, you will turn slightly onto your left side as your right shoulder begins to open up. You are taking a breath as your right hand is ending its underwater phase and exiting the water at your hip. Then, as your right hand is recovering and going back toward the front of the stroke, your body is rotating back into the water, with your head coming with it.

Every time your head turns, your body will turn, so you do not want excessive movement from either. For example, if your head turns 45 degrees, we want to see your body rotate about 45 degrees as well. Aim to keep rotation between 45 and 60 degrees, no more. Overrotation causes misalignment by creating a banana-shaped body, wide leg spread, and slowing cadence. Your body's rotation should ideally be equal on both sides, right and left, although it's not uncommon to have slightly more rotation or unevenness toward the preferred breathing side. In fact, this might be desirable for open-water swimming. For example, in choppy, turbulent conditions, you could be faced with waves hitting you on your left side. If you have

CORRECT When rotation is controlled, breathing is more likely to be short and crisp.

INCORRECT Overrotation causes misalignment, a wider kick, and slower cadence.

Lifting the head to sight typically means the hips and legs drop, so it is important to make the process of sighting as smooth, elegant, and easy to execute as possible.

only trained to breathe to your left side, you are going to have real problems successfully taking a breath in these conditions. This is why it is so important to be able to breathe to both sides.

We must be mindful that triathletes are open-water swimmers, which means we must be able to lift our heads for sighting, both for navigation and awareness. This has an effect on breathing and alignment because it disrupts head position, but it is a necessary part of open-water swimming. It means we need to be able to build sighting into our breathing pattern with minimal disruption to head position, alignment, and body position. Lifting the head to sight typically means the hips and legs drop, so it is important to make the process of sighting as smooth, elegant, and easy to execute as possible. Chapter 8 will cover the skill of sighting in more detail.

BREATHING AND RACING

Breathing is one of the first functions of the human body affected when we experience anxiety and nerves. Most triathletes experience an increased breathing rate or shortness of breath when they are anxious. This is especially common before and during the swim start of a race and more intense for those inexperienced with open-water swimming. All of these issues are compounded by the fact that triathletes are almost always wearing a wet suit on race day, which can restrict the chest, leading to greater difficulties with breathing, especially in cold water.

RACE-READY BREATHING | Protocol

▸ Practice your warm-up routine in training so it feels familiar on race day. I sometimes "surprise" athletes when they show up for a workout. Instead of prescribing a swim warm-up, I tell them they have 10 minutes to warm up on dry land before we do a 20-minute time trial. This is great practice for race day.

▸ Practice swimming in your wet suit to get comfortable with how it feels. Make sure it is not too tight. If you don't have the opportunity to swim in it before race day, soak it overnight in the bathtub. This will help loosen it up slightly so you can break it in more easily.

▸ Practice race takeout speed. The excitement of race day often leads to fast, high-intensity swimming from the moment the gun goes off, regardless of whether you intended to start the race this way. If you haven't trained for this, you will undoubtedly suffer for it. Just because it is race day doesn't mean your body will suddenly be able to reach new heights of performance. If you want to see race-day magic happen, then you need to practice race-day magic. Get familiar with the discomfort in training so you can effectively execute it when it's time to perform.

▸ On race day, always warm up, preferably in the water. If there is no opportunity for a pre-race swim warm-up, do a dry-land warm-up. An 8–10-minute jog with light mobility exercises such as arm swings, shoulder shrugs, and freestyle strokes is a good alternative to elevate your heart rate and begin working up a sweat.

▸ If your race is taking place in cold weather, and the water temperature is expected to be cold, you should prepare accordingly. If the water is 60 degrees Fahrenheit or cooler, then do not execute an in-water swim warm-up prior to the race start. Instead, do an 8–10-minute jog in your wet suit, making sure to get your core warm, your blood flowing, and your heart rate elevated. Execute some reps with stretch cords if they have been part of your training routine. Take time to adapt to the water temperature: Splash some water on your face and body and dunk your head in the water a few times. This will help combat the shortness of breath and "brain freeze" that often comes from getting into colder water.

To be "race ready" you need to know how to cope with these feelings when they occur, replicating them in practice so you are more familiar with them on race day. This is one of the reasons I believe race day warm-ups are so important. When the gun goes off, if your body is not well warmed up, then the sudden increase in heart rate, effort, and adrenaline can often lead to shortness of breath, an anxiety attack, or worse for some swimmers. You want to set yourself up for success by managing the variables that can affect your breathing.

6

Kicking

TO KICK OR NOT TO KICK; that is the question. When it comes to swimming for triathlon, kicking can be a double-edged sword and a topic that can be confusing, controversial, and misunderstood. What is the value of kicking? How do you train it? How much should you train it? These are all valid questions, often asked by triathlon swimmers and astute coaches.

When it comes to assessing the purpose, value, and return expected of kicking, the differences between the demands of competitive swimming and those of triathlon become even more magnified. In competitive swimming, approximately 85 percent of races are two minutes or less, and 95 percent of races are five minutes or less. In triathlon, the shortest open-water swim time you might encounter would be around 10 minutes for a faster athlete racing a sprint-distance event. Particularly for long-distance triathlons such as Ironman, we are looking at a swim duration of an hour or maybe even two hours for some.

My fellow Tower 26 coach and podcast partner, Jim Lubinski, happens to be a former pro hockey player. He likens the common practice of training triathletes to be good swimmers to the suggestion that a hockey player and a figure skater could prepare in the same way. Although both athletes perform on ice, the demands of the two sports are obviously different. It's easy to see how the experience and perspective of a traditional swimming coach could vary significantly from that of a triathlon swim coach.

KICKING AND PROPULSION

With traditional swimming events being so short in duration, the propulsive value of the kick can be extremely high. The race is over in a matter of minutes, and it does not matter if the legs are taxed at the end. For this reason, a lot of traditional swim coaches are fierce advocates of the need to develop a strong, propulsive kick. Kick sets are quite rightly a valuable part of training for these events.

In triathlon, when athletes exit the water, they still have about 80–90 percent of their race remaining, all of which is hugely dependent on their legs. For the majority of triathletes, the benefits of taxing the legs come at too high a cost, especially as most are poor kickers and tend to kick from the knee rather than the hip. Those coaches advising triathletes to spend time on kicking are most likely looking at it from the perspective of competitive swimming. If you are a triathlete looking to improve your swimming, propulsive kicking should be at the lower end of your list of priorities.

Benefits of Kicking

Although kicking is less valuable in triathlon, I'm not suggesting you disregard it completely. It plays a critical role in understanding and executing tautness in the water, the foundation of stroke mechanics. Many benefits come from building this skill, so you'll find that kicking is prevalent in our program, but the approach or volume differs from what you would find in a traditional swimming program.

For starters, kicking helps to promote ankle flexibility, particularly when wearing fins. Triathletes are notoriously stiff in the ankles, especially those who come from a running background. For this reason, the majority of the kicking in our workouts involves fins.

Done correctly, kicking can also help to promote recovery. Most age-group tri-athletes have a disproportionately high training volume over the weekend, leaving their legs heavy and tired. Kicking helps flush the fatigue and expedite muscle repair and recovery.

If you lack fluidity in your stroke, kicking with fins can often help, giving you an added boost of propulsion and developing your proprioceptive feel for moving through the water.

Disadvantages of Kicking

I won't sugarcoat it: Most triathletes are terrible at kicking. It might take 90 seconds or more to kick 50 meters, so kick sets burn through a lot of training time, far from ideal for those with a limited time budget. In short, it is not going to optimize the triathlete's time investment.

The mechanics of kicking present another challenge for the triathlete. Enlisting most of the large muscle groups in the legs—the hamstrings, quadriceps, and glutes—kicking also comes at a fairly high aerobic cost. Heart rate can go up quickly. Is it worth it? Will race performance be compromised? The answer is most likely yes, your race performance will be affected.

If you are not a good kicker and have not yet developed tautness, kicking can cause a lot of vibration through your upper body and result in displaced energy and directional force. This means you might notice your body rocking from side to side or up and down—in fact, any movement other than forward movement. Vibration is created if your frame is not taut, so a swimmer who has an appreciation for taut-ness will likely be a better kicker than one who has not developed this yet.

KICKING AND TRIATHLON

Kicking for triathlon swimmers is a balancing act: Do it wrong, and it will cost you dearly, but do it well, and it may aid propulsion. We cannot categorically say that kicking is a must in swimming for triathlon, but we cannot count it out completely.

Interestingly, some triathletes who have no background in swimming are innately great kickers. The power and propulsion they can generate from their legs is impressive and well worth capitalizing on. With these athletes, I like to maintain kicking to keep the benefits there but not overuse it. I must add that these triathletes are few and far between. The majority of triathletes could spend a lot of time trying to generate propulsion from kicking and still fall short of the mark. In my opinion, it is far wiser and safer for triathletes not to have the propulsive element of their stroke rely on their legs.

We often see triathletes with weird habits when it comes to kicking: legs spread too wide, scissor kicking, too much amplitude, too much knee bend, or flexed feet. The best outcome we can aim for is to have stabilized legs, gentle kicking, narrow amplitude, and ankles never too far away from each other. We want to see the upbeat and the downbeat of the kick remain within a narrow range, keeping it soft and gentle. If you can do these things, then you are going to minimize any negative value from leg usage. If the kick is too wide or too big, then it can hurt propulsion and have a detrimental effect on drag and velocity, that is, the speed at which you move through the water.

The only exception to this is for professional triathletes, especially those racing on the ITU circuit, where having sharp takeout speed is essential and a strong, propulsive kick can help generate this.

When swimming with a kickboard, always wear a snorkel so your head can stay down, creating a flat body line rather than one angled with the water's surface. Your arms are extended in front of you, holding the kickboard at the bottom or sides toward the bottom. The three touch points—back of the head, butt, and heels—should all be at the surface of the water and the body flat and taut. The goal is a stable upper body, without excessive movement or rocking. When you do it correctly, you will really feel the propulsive effect of your kick moving you forward.

After you have developed a feel for this, then you can progress to kicking without fins, but you should rarely do more than 50-meter efforts, with the same set-up: arms outstretched holding a kickboard at the bottom, snorkel on, and face down in the water. Keep a high-cadence kick, kicking from the hip, not the knee. After you master this, you can start to add some speed and intensity.

Note that we only progress skills when the basic foundation of technique has been established. When you feel comfortable performing the skill, then it's time to move on. Far too often I see novice triathletes in the pool who have heard about the benefits of kicking on their side, so they attempt to make it from one end of the pool to the other. It looks like torture, and they are almost drowning! This is a perfect example of an advanced drill that requires a sound technical platform in order to execute well. Doing it without that platform causes them to struggle, devaluing the drill and their time. If you are going to try kicking on your side, at least do so following the same protocol as you would for vertical kicking, ensuring your body is taut, straight, and aligned, and you are wearing fins. Far more preferable would be to follow our kicking guidelines instead with sensible skill progression. You might spend upward of 30 percent of your workout on skills like these in the Technical Phase, but that percentage decreases in the training phases that follow.

KICKING PROPERLY | Keys

- ▶ Point and turn your toes inward. Keep your ankles close as well.
- ▶ As you draw your heels toward the surface (up kick), bend your knees slightly.
- ▶ As you down kick, straighten your legs, engaging both hip flexors and quads in this main propulsive phase.
- ▶ With your legs kicking independently, keep the amplitude reasonably narrow— no wider than your shoulders.
- ▶ Execute kicking at a high cadence rate, but keep the effort rather gentle. Because kicking sends vibration upward toward the torso, stabilize your upper body to prevent it from rocking side to side.

Because proper kicking technique is fundamental to establishing tautness, you will recognize some of these drills from the 10-step tautness progression in Chapter 4. Here we will focus just on kicking and expound on some of the finer points of the technique, which could prove to be a good use of your time after you have mastered tautness.

Step 1: Kick with fins and front-mounted snorkel, thumbs interlaced, no board

The focus is on the three surface touch points and a taut frame that is stretched, long, and sleek. This is the optimal body posture you want to achieve and maintain, the foundation for faster swimming.

Interlace your thumbs, palms facing the bottom of the pool, with hands approximately 2–4 inches beneath the water's surface. Extend your arms in front of you so your body becomes stretched out, securing a long, taut frame with your biceps squeezing your ears.

Put your face in the water with the tip of your nose pointing toward the bottom of the pool. The surface of the water should be at the top of your head, where your spine would protrude if it extended out of your head.

Ensure that you have three touch points with the water's surface: the back of your head, your butt, and your heels. Maintain these three touch points at all times. They are the first things to break down when fatigue sets in.

Step 2: Butterfly kick on your back with fins

The Tower 26 method includes a lot of butterfly kicking on your back in the open-water skill-building and race-ready phases. It's the most specific development of core strength for open-water swimmers and triathletes.

Place hands one on top of the other, with palms facing downward and fingers together. Take the thumb of your top hand and wrap it under the palm of your lower hand. If poor flexibility prevents this, interlace your thumbs and hold your hands a couple of inches apart.

Extend your arms as far above your head as possible. Try squeezing your ears with your biceps, shaping your body like an arrow. This lengthens your body to create a taut posture.

Turn over onto your back and start kicking, with your outstretched arms resting on the water's surface. Kick both legs simultaneously, with your knees and ankles together, never separated.

Try to keep your hips at the surface and the tips of your fins touching the water's surface as you kick. Don't let your knees break the surface of the water. Keep the amplitude of your kicks reasonably narrow—no wider than your shoulders.

The kick originates from your core and hip flexors, not the knees. Move your legs downward by mainly using your hip flexors and hamstrings, with minor glute engagement. As you draw your leg down, introduce a small knee bend with your toes pointed. Begin the up kick by returning your legs toward the water's surface, straightening your knee. Your quad engagement occurs here, with your toes pointed and your ankles relaxed.

Step 3: Kick on your back with or without fins

Place your hands one on top of the other, palms facing downward and fingers together. Wrap the thumb of your top palm around your lower hand's palm. Holding your hands in that position, extend your arms as far above your head as possible. Squeeze your ears with your biceps, shaping your body like an arrow to lengthen it and create a taut posture.

Turn over on your back and start kicking, with your outstretched arms resting on the water's surface. Try to keep your hips at the surface and the tips of your fins (or toes if not wearing fins) touching the water's surface as you kick. Don't let your knees break the water's surface. Keep the amplitude of your kick reasonably narrow—no wider than your shoulders.

The kick originates from the hip flexors, not the knees. Move your leg downward by mainly using your hip flexors and hamstrings, with minor glute engagement. As you draw down your leg, introduce a small knee bend with your toes pointed. Start the up kick by returning your leg toward the water's surface, straightening your knee. Your quad engagement occurs here, with your toes pointed and your ankle relaxed.

Step 4: Kick with a board and snorkel, no fins

Hold the kickboard either with your hands positioned on the sides of the board or resting on top of the bottom part of the board. Extend your arms, securing a long, taut frame with your biceps squeezing your ears. Keep your face in the water with the tip of your nose pointing toward the bottom of the pool. The water level should be at the top of your head.

You should have three touch points with the water's surface: the back of your head, butt, and heels. Maintain these three touch points at all times. They are the first things to break down when fatigue sets in.

Have your toes pointed and turned inward, and begin kicking your legs independently. As you draw your heel toward the surface (up kick), bend your knees slightly. As you down kick, straighten your leg, engaging both your hip flexor and quad in this main propulsive phase. Keep the amplitude of your kick reasonably narrow—no wider than your shoulders. Execute kicking with a high cadence rate.

Because kicking sends a vibration upward toward the torso, stabilize your upper body to prevent it from rocking side to side.

Remember, flexible ankles lead to increased propulsion. It's important to make sure your body position remains intact. This way, everyone improves! Remember that some triathletes may never see improved flexibility; instead they just learn to point their feet and toes.

Step 5: Kick with a snorkel and no board or fins

Interlace your thumbs, palms facing the bottom of the pool, with hands approximately 1–2 inches beneath the water's surface.

Extend your arms in front of you, securing a long, taut frame with your biceps squeezing your ears. Keep your face in the water with the tip of your nose pointing toward the bottom of the pool. The water level should be at the top of your head. Keep your head completely still.

Ensure that you have three touch points with the water's surface: the back of your head, butt, and heels. Maintain these touch points at all times—these will be the first things to break down when fatigue sets in.

Have your toes pointed and turned inward as you start kicking with a high cadence. As you draw your heels toward the surface (up kick), bend your knees slightly. As you down kick, straighten your leg, engaging both hip flexors and quads in this main propulsive phase. Keep the amplitude of your kick reasonably narrow—no wider than your shoulders. Because kicking sends a vibration upward toward the torso, stabilize your upper body to prevent it from rocking side to side.

Advanced technique: Kick on your side with fins, no snorkel

Extend your lower arm straight out in front of you, with your palm facing toward the pool floor. Your hand should be approximately 2–4 inches beneath the water's surface, directly in line with your shoulder. Your opposite arm should be at your side, resting comfortably on your hip or leg.

Hold your body in a rotated position, between 45 and 60 degrees at most. Press your jaw or cheek against the inside of your shoulder, with no gap between them, holding your head in a fixed position.

Arm fully extended with hand 2–4 inches beneath the surface.

Palm facing downward.

No gap between cheek and shoulder.

To breathe, turn your head only enough for your mouth to clear the water and inhale. Turn your head back into the water, eyes looking downward, cheek tucked against your shoulder.

Turn your head to breathe without rotating your torso or hips. Keep your head close to your shoulder, maintaining only a small gap between head and shoulder, if any, as you turn your head to the side to breathe. Make crisp, short head turns—after inhalation, immediately return your head back to its fixed position. When you turn your head to breathe, there should be no lifting, no tucking, no tilting—just turning. Employ a narrow kick, keeping your body in a straight line.

7

Swim-Specific Strength and Mobility

THERE ARE NO SHORTCUTS to improved performance, but over the years I have come to see how adding activation, mobility, and strength work to training can be a conduit for more efficient movement as well as injury prevention. One of the biggest factors in achieving improvement is consistency, yet one of the greatest enemies of consistency is injury. When it comes to adding swim-specific strength and mobility to your training, we want to keep it as simple as possible. Asking an already time-crunched triathlete to spend an extra two hours in the gym each week is neither smart nor sustainable. If you are adding a fourth discipline to your triathlon training program, the work has to be absolutely essential, intelligently mapped out, and time efficient.

I am fortunate to have worked with some tremendous strength coaches and movement experts in recent years, including Erin Carson, a strength and conditioning coach with more than 25 years' experience in the field as well as a talented and passionate age-group triathlete herself. She has overseen the strength program of three-time Ironman world champion Mirinda Carfrae since 2013, in addition to many other elite and age-group athletes in Boulder, Colorado, and her ECFit strength programs are available at ecfitstrength.com. Teaming up with experts to leverage resources is something I have always valued as a coach, and I've been happy to direct athletes toward Erin's strength program, included here.

Erin developed a swim-specific strength program for Tower 26 athletes that incorporates both mobility and strength work. In addition to the stretch cords work I ask all of my athletes to do, the mobility work can be done poolside before a swim workout to help activate and engage the major muscle groups needed for efficient swimming. The strength work can be done away from the pool, either in a gym or at home, and aims to help stimulate and improve the strength and efficiency of the major muscles used while swimming.

ACTIVATION WORK

Dry-Land Tubing

Stretch cords (tubing) are an extremely efficient way of activating your body for swimming, firing up your shoulders, arms, and lats before you hit the water. They are also perfect for race day.

I ask athletes to arrive 10–15 minutes before practice starts in order to warm up. This typically entails three sets of 30–100 reps, with quantity depending on season timing, resting as needed between sets. If you are just starting out with stretch cords, do three sets of 30 reps, adding 10 reps each week. Of course, you need to ensure you are executing the technique correctly because it is easy to get wrong. Follow the guidelines for optimal technique; there is also a video demonstration on the Tower 26 YouTube channel (Bands Demo).

Make sure you have the appropriate resistance for your strength. If you are new to tubing exercises, start with light resistance. Attach the tubing to a fixed object at waist height—the poles and ladders at the pool work well.

Tubing drill, 3 sets of 30–100 reps

Place your hands in the paddles and step back until the tubing is taut. Bend at the waist, allowing your torso to become almost parallel to the ground, keeping a slight bend in your knees. Set up for start position with your arms outstretched but not fully extended. Bend your elbow at approximately 120 degrees, with light tension on the band and your fingertips pointed at the ground.

Begin executing your stroke with a firm wrist, either moving both arms together or alternating. Throughout the stroke, ensure your elbows remain pointed outward and elevated above your wrists. Focus on accelerating your hand backward while keeping your fingertips pointed to the floor. This is a quick movement.

Return to the start position and then repeat. Rest as needed between sets.

Initiating the set-up (left). Concluding the set-up (center). Concluding propulsive phase (right).

After completing the pull, recover by releasing the tension in the tubing as you lower your arms down and back to the start position.

Mobility

A few minutes spent looking after basic mobility can pay great dividends when it comes to staying healthy, remaining injury free, and performing better. Of course, the type of work you undertake if going into a full strength and conditioning program can vary greatly based on your background, injury history, gender, age, and time available to train.

These exercises are quick and simple and involve body weight only. The arm and shoulder movements should be performed against a wall, paying particular attention to keeping your lower back flat against the wall. You want to do all you can to keep your pelvis in a neutral position. Your lats can become extremely tight from swimming, and when that occurs, they will pull on your lower back, creating an arch. These exercise movements help to activate the back of your body, known as the posterior chain.

Double-arm overhead raise, 10 reps

Stand with your back, head, and shoulders against the wall, heels about a foot apart. With your thumbs pointing straight up, raise both arms over your head, making sure your lower back remains connected to the wall. Your arms should be moving perpendicular to

the wall and then straight up overhead, ending with your thumbs facing the wall. If it's not possible to reach your arms overhead while keeping your back in contact with the wall, then just move your arms as far as you can. Return your arms to the start position, and repeat.

Alternate arm overhead raise, 10 reps on each side

Set up is the same as the double-arm overhead raise, but instead of raising both arms, do one left-arm raise, then one right-arm raise to count as one rep.

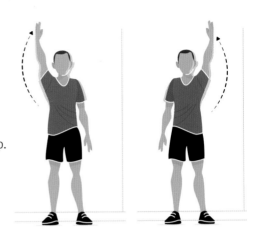

Backstroke arms, 1 minute

Imagine you're swimming backstroke on the pool deck, vigorously circling your arms backward to get the blood flowing and open up your chest. Swimming freestyle for an hour or more during an intense workout leads to the front side of the body closing up and the muscles shortening, so moving your arms backward really helps to open up that

front side and counteract this. Try to include some backstroke swimming in your easy swims and cooldown, too.

• • •

Just three to five minutes of these exercises prior to swimming will really help activate your posterior chain. We want all of these muscles to be activated and ready for swimming as soon as you dive in. If you don't get to this prior to your swim, start your gym work with these mobility exercises.

THE ECFIT TOWER 26 STRENGTH PROGRAM

One of the greatest benefits of strength work is making your body more robust, efficient, and resilient so that it can withstand all the training load that lies ahead. As Erin says, consistent strength work translates to making speed feel easier—that is, hard work doesn't feel as hard.

Erin knows the sport, having excelled as an age-group triathlete. Her passion and experience result in strength and conditioning programs that help triathletes stay strong, mobile, and agile. She acknowledges there are a number of training variables that affect the architecture of athletes' strength programs; for example, how much weight, how many sets, how many repetitions, how long, and when in their training week they can hit the gym.

However, before any strength training can begin, it is imperative that athletes are moving well. That means no pain or visible motor dysfunctions in their movements. The goal is to get athletes lifting as heavy a load as possible without injury or mistakes. This might take longer for some people than for others.

For older athletes, strength work can become even more important than it was in their younger days. Gravity can be both our biggest asset and enemy in staying healthy, working against us to pull us out of alignment. Understanding strength and mobility work is about understanding how to load our skeletal, fascial, and muscular systems to the extent that we won't succumb to gravity and time.

Low-plank hold, 1 minute

In a prone (face-down) position, hold your body off the ground with your upper body supported on your elbows. It is important to keep your head in a strong position, similar to the one you would hold while swimming. Engage your core.

Low-plank rotations, 10 reps on each side

From the low plank position, rotate your trunk to gently rock your hips from side to side. Engage your core to control the movement and keep the rest of the body, your lower body and shoulders, stationary.

T-spine rotations, 10 reps on each side

From a quadruped position (hands and knees), place one hand on the back of your head, and gently rotate your elbow from a low to high position. When your shoulders are "stacked," focus on stretching and opening your chest.

Lat pull-down, 2 sets of 10 reps, moderate load

Begin in a strong postural position, with your chest high. Pull the high cable bar to your chest. Return the bar to starting position with control. Note: Lift your chest to meet the bar for an enhanced lat contraction.

Seated row, 2 sets of 10 reps, moderate load

Start again from a strong postural position, with your chest proud. Pull the horizontal cable bar in toward your rib cage. Return the bar to starting position with control. Feel your scapulas come together, shoulders remain down and back.

**Alternate plank reaches,
2 sets of 10 reps on each side**

From a prone plank position, gently reach out in front of you with one arm and then the other. Keep your head in the same position as it would be while swimming. One arm reach equals one rep.

Stability ball single-arm dumbbell chest press, 2 sets of 10 reps

Lie on a stability ball face up, with your head and neck supported by the ball. Your hips should be high and glutes engaged. With a dumbbell in one arm and hips high, press the dumbbell toward the ceiling.

Single-arm single-leg row, 10 reps on each side

Stand on one leg and hold a dumbbell in the opposite hand. Hinge forward from the hips and pull the weight in toward your rib cage. As you lower the weight keep your core strong and upper body steady. Note: Your right shoulder has a significant connection with your left hip and vice versa, so you want to awaken these connections and get things firing. This helps immensely with your hip rotation when in the water as well as maintaining a tight core, which ultimately aids in tautness, alignment, and propulsion.

Single-arm lat pull-down, 2 sets of 10 reps on each side, moderate load

Sit tall and grip a high cable with one arm. Some rotation can be incorporated into this strong pull to the bottom of your ribs. Be sure to keep your shoulder down to ensure great lat contraction.

Single-leg single-arm standing row, 2 sets of 10 reps on each side

Standing on one leg, hold the handle of a horizontal cable with the opposite hand. Keeping your shoulder low, pull the handle toward the bottom of your rib cage. Let your torso open up as you release back to the starting position.

• • •

It is sometimes difficult to know when to add strength work to your weekly triathlon training. If you are a time-crunched age-group athlete, then it is best to add 20 minutes of mobility and stability work to your easy day. Try adding strength work to days that already have higher intensity work scheduled. Gym work can be hard on the body, and we want to make sure the hard days stay hard and the easy days remain easy.

Try to ensure your strength work comes after your sports-specific session, not before it, so that you are not fatigued going into your key swim, bike, or run workout. This also means your body is typically warmed up when you hit the gym later in the day, and you'll have greater mobility. Strength training is a supporting activity, not the bull's-eye activity. Rule of thumb: Don't compromise key sessions by doing anything that could detract from that day's optimal training.

Erin typically sees some of the pro triathletes after a key swim workout, which means they might not need to do a lot of mobility work. Instead, they can go straight into stability work, such as low planks, high planks, and single-leg exercises—something to engage the body prior to lifting.

Strength and mobility work should always be designed to enhance your swim, bike, and run workouts. Investing even the smallest amount of time and effort each week into making your body stronger, more agile, and more stable will translate to improved training, greater consistency, and ultimately better performance. Just be sure to optimize your time as outlined.

8

Mastering Open Water

SWIMMING IN OPEN WATER is dynamic and demanding. It involves learning a wide range of skills, and it can be intimidating and challenging, even for those with years of experience. When I see photos from the swim starts of triathlon races, it never comes as a surprise to me to see so many anxious faces. I can tell what many of these athletes are thinking: "Just get this swim over with and let me get to my bike."

It doesn't need to be like that. You can and will enjoy all three parts of your race if you learn the right open-water swimming skills and hone them in training. Regardless of your age, ability, experience, or fitness, there is absolutely no reason you cannot line up for a race with the utmost confidence. We like to call it being race ready. It will take some hard work and commitment, but you can be prepared for whatever the open water throws at you.

Perhaps the most important factor to remember is that training for an open-water swim is not the same as training for an event in the pool. That might seem obvious, but it is staggering to me how many triathletes think they can train year-round in a pool and then, as if by magic, be able to handle open-water swimming. The two environments could not be more different. In the pool, you are in a fixed environment with lane lines, a constant temperature, and static conditions. In open water, the variables are significant: You can face cold water, strong currents, high surf, foggy conditions, dark water, and marine life, to name but a few. If you only ever swim in a pool, then you will be ill-equipped to cope with the many demands of open-water swimming. To perform optimally in open water, you also need to feel comfortable and confident with beach starts, in-water starts, swimming in close proximity with others (often with physical contact), turning around buoys, drafting, sighting, dolphin diving, and exiting the water. As I'm sure you can tell, learning to master open water means learning to master a wide range of skills. Not all of these skills must be learned or always practiced in open water; many can be honed in the pool and transferred across, but the salient point here is that you do need to acquire and practice them. Simply swimming up and down in a pool, without including some or all of the skills listed above, is not setting you up for optimal success come race day. You need to get acquainted with all the variables that open water will throw at you. The process of moving from fear to familiarity requires frequent preparation. You might well have a number of fears about open-water swimming, and most people do. By frequently practicing key open-water skills, you build familiarity and adaptation, which at the very least reduce your fears and make the entire process abundantly easier.

The anxiety and fear athletes experience around open-water swimming should not be underestimated. Even the most experienced and talented swimmers have significant fears about swimming in open water, whether it's in the ocean, a lake, or a river. Respect your fears and acknowledge them, but also understand that you can work through them. Remember that no one is entirely fearless. I have been swimming in open water since the age of 11, and even now in my 50s, I still have my hesitations. I am not the greatest fan of physical contact while racing, I'm not keen on being in a crowded space in the water, I definitely do not like being unable to see the bottom of the ocean or lake in which I'm swimming, and certain types of marine life still make me nervous! But during the course of the many hundreds of open-water workouts I've done in my lifetime, I have grown familiar with all of these things— and more. I wouldn't say I'm 100 percent comfortable with all of them even now, but

I've grown to accept them as part of open-water swimming. Familiarity breeds comfort, and with adequate preparation, comfort brings confidence.

The good news is that acquiring the necessary skills and becoming familiar with these discomforts does not need to be complicated. Even if you have limited access to open water, you can include most of the key skills into your training in the pool. In my experience, most athletes can learn a new skill if they practice it 10 times consistently over three weeks. This can vary based on athletes' aptitude and experience, but for the most part this is the standard pattern. At Tower 26, we begin introducing some of these skills into our pool workouts after we reach the open-water skill-building phase in early May.

OPEN-WATER SKILL-BUILDING PHASE

The open-water skill-building phase is vital in the multistage, year-round approach we take to training. Although I place great value on all stages of our plan, if pressed to do so I would say this phase above all others is the most important. If you had only three months in which to train, I would strongly urge you to follow the demands of this phase. It includes a massive injection of so many of the key ingredients of open-water swimming and racing: endurance, skill, and power as well as the basic mechanics of proper swimming. On top of this, we layer in all the specifics of open-water swimming: sighting, drafting, pacing, turning, entries and exits, handling different water and air temperatures, currents, and marine life. In short, we leave no stone unturned so that you can approach race day brimming with confidence.

Sighting

It astounds me that what is perhaps the most important skill for open-water swimming is one that triathletes tend to avoid practicing. Good, effective sighting can mean the difference between swimming the 1.2-mile course you are intended to follow in a 70.3 race or swimming 1.5 miles by mistake. Given how easy it is to learn and practice, I know which option our athletes prefer! The key to sighting is doing it frequently. Many athletes will take 20 or 30 single-arm strokes before lifting their heads to check if they are still on course. That is simply too many strokes. In the time it takes to swim 30 strokes, it is extremely likely you will swim off course. Many of us have asymmetries or muscular imbalances that can lead to veering slightly to the left or right, even though it might feel as though we are swimming in a perfectly straight line. For this reason, take no more than 6 to 10 strokes (with a stroke being defined as a single arm movement), sight, and then repeat. The exact number of strokes to take between sightings is hugely dependent on conditions. If you are swimming in placid, lake-like conditions and the course is well marked with easy-to-spot buoys, then sighting every 10 strokes should be adequate. If you are in choppy or foggy conditions, then you should certainly be sighting every 6 strokes, perhaps even more frequently. In many professional ITU races or in the front pack of professional Ironman races, it is not uncommon to see athletes sighting more frequently, every 2 to 4 strokes. Sighting needs to be built into the mechanics of the stroke—this is vital. You want to be able to sight frequently without it having any impact on performance.

A few different methods of sighting, such as crocodile eyes and water-polo style, can be effective for more advanced swimmers but are not ideal for triathlon racing. Crocodile eyes involves lifting your eyes just barely above the water line. It is highly ineffective in a dynamic, open-water environment and never recommended

At left, crocodile eyes sighting (a quick, efficient lift of the head) is ineffective in a dynamic environment. At right, water-polo sighting (sustained through a full stroke cycle) is less efficient in open-water swimming.

Practice sighting in the pool to improve efficiency. Lift your head high enough to be prepared for open-water conditions.

unless in a pool triathlon or in flat, lake-like conditions. Water-polo-style sighting involves a string of continuous arm strokes while keeping your head elevated above the water. Although this style is more effective than crocodile eyes, it typically impedes your speed at a greater rate.

The sight-and-breathe method I teach is widely considered the most efficient, and with enough practice requires the least energy to incorporate into your stroke. If you are a right-sided breather, you initiate head lifting as your left hand is exiting the water. As your left hand finishes its stroke, and your arm is being lifted out of the water, there is a slight lift of the left side of your body—your elbow and arm are coming out of the water—and that lift occurs simultaneously with your initiation of the head lift. As your left arm starts to come over and around to reenter the water, your head is lifted, and in that time your eyes, nose, and sometimes mouth clear the water line. You want to lift your head just enough to capture a snapshot of information before your left hand reenters the water and your head turns to the right to capture a breath in its regular routine. This is not a mechanical movement but a smooth, fluid one that takes place in just a fraction of a second: lift, sight, breathe, lift, sight, breathe. You capture the breath as your head is turning to the right, then put your head back into the water and continue like this for 6, 8, or 10 single strokes before sighting again.

The most common problem with sighting is that most athletes do not practice it enough. It is a simple skill but must be built into training with high frequency at every session during race season. It should become an established part of your

Combine sighting with breathing in a fluid motion to further maximize efficiency.

swim stroke mechanics so that it becomes no effort at all. If you are racing an Iron-man, which involves a 2.4-mile swim, you are likely going to sight around 400 times during the course of that swim. If you haven't practiced sighting, then during your swim it will soon become an arduous task that results in high muscular fatigue, typically in the upper neck and lower back. This is far from ideal before getting on your bike for a 112-mile ride.

I am often asked what you should do if you sight and do not actually see any-thing. Of course, if the water is choppy, then we might sight several times and see nothing but the water turbulence directly in front of us. That is not a sighting. In this case, you would need to repeat the action again on the very next stroke, lifting your head slightly higher, until you do see something. If you still draw a blank after three to four successive tries, you might need to slow down or even stop to look around. This would be a last resort and is obviously not preferable.

Pack Swimming

Pool workouts are usually very orderly, and most pool swimmers strictly adhere to lane etiquette. When it comes to open-water swimming, there are no such rules, and expecting your swim to be similar to a pool workout will lead to a few surprises. In the pool, there is rarely contact between swimmers. Athletes are always spread out, leaving a 5–10-second gap between each other. Being put into a race environment where you can have more than two thousand swimmers vying for the same space at the same time is obviously a very different experience. Getting familiar with it can be easily practiced in the pool and is something I like to do at our pool workouts. We remove the lane lines, creating an open space, and might put 10 or 12 swimmers in one lane, positioning them in three rows. We execute a lot of 25-yard/meter intervals like this, with the swimmers switching positions after two or three repeats so they know what it is like to have people all around them. After all, you cannot always dictate where you will be positioned on race day, but eventually, with the right skills and experience, you can learn to manipulate and manage your position within the pack.

It is not uncommon to hear triathletes' war stories from swim start lines. "I was smacked in the face" or "I was punched in the neck" are not unfamiliar post-race anecdotes. I firmly believe the physical contact that often takes place during the swim, especially during the swim start, is not intentional. It is the result of a lot of highly energized, adrenalized competitors all vying for space in extremely close quarters. Arms and legs are thrashing around, and it is next to impossible for the person next to you not to hit or bump you. There is little you can do about this, but what you can do is get familiar with it. You might never grow comfortable with it, but you can change your mindset so you are less reactive when you do experience physical contact and be more proactive about seeking open space. You do not want

to train to hit the person who hits you; rather, you want to train to cope with being hit and continuing without undue stress or unnecessary reactions. The best way to do this is to train under these circumstances. Learning to breathe through it, not react aggressively, and continue focusing on your own swimming will help make race swim starts far less aggravating.

Drafting

Drafting can be hugely important, particularly in elite-level racing, and it can have its place in age-group racing, too. The key to maximizing drafting is knowing when it can be beneficial because there are certainly times when it is not. There can be tremendous benefits to drafting on the feet or hips of faster swimmers, but the benefits depreciate significantly for athletes swimming over 1:30 per 100 meters. With slower triathletes, it is also more likely their open-water skill set is not as advanced, so you run the risk of trying to draft off someone who has limited ability to navigate effectively, and you blindly follow them off course. The best option is to always be your own navigator and mark your own course.

Drafting is important for the top 20 percent of athletes, and it's all about knowing where and when to draft. The most commonly practiced approach is swimming with your fingertips as close as possible to the feet in front of you. Continually tap-

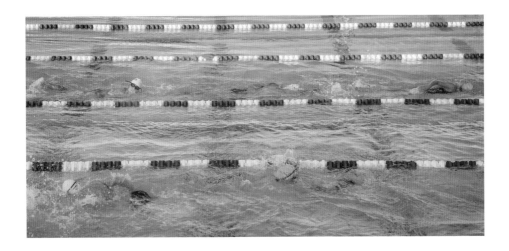

ping those feet can become incredibly annoying for that swimmer, and you could find yourself on the receiving end of some short, sharp kicks to try to deter you, so the best practice is to stay there and make contact as little as possible. It is estimated that drafting in this position just off the feet of the swimmer in front will yield about a 3 percent savings in energy. Drafting just off the hip yields about a 7 percent energy saving, but this position can be harder to attain. If drafting off the hip, you will be in a lot closer contact with that swimmer, and many athletes won't like you being there, not least because it gives them the feeling of being sucked back while you slingshot forward. Because of the position of their hand and elbow as they bring their arm out of the water to recover, you also stand a good chance of being hit, so you need to be prepared for this. If you can get it right, though, there is a sweet spot while drafting off the hip that garners great energy saving with minimal contact. As with all of these skills, it requires continued practice in training to get it right in racing.

Pace Lining

I really enjoy building pace lining into workouts. It is the swimming version of the drafting you commonly see in cycling races, in which athletes position themselves in a single line, one behind the other, with the lead athlete doing the lion's share of

the work. Those athletes sitting in positions No. 2, No. 3, No. 4, and beyond are enjoying the free speed while doing significantly less work. We practice this a lot in the pool, usually with four athletes all swimming one behind the other and switching the lead every 50 or 100 yards/meters. Only after you've done it a few times do you have the "a-ha" moment about "sitting in" and staying on the swimmer's feet in front of you.

As an example, let's say we have a group of four swimmers who, when swimming at 80 percent effort, would usually clock around 1:30 pace per 100 meters. The four of them all push off in close proximity to each other, with the leader swimming at 1:30 pace. The thought processes of each of these swimmers typically goes like this:

Swimmer 1: "Wow, I'm swimming so hard—this is so much faster than 1:30 pace, I'm going to drop all of these guys. Suckers!"

Swimmer 2: "This is nice and comfortable; this feels quite slow. I wonder if the leader is even trying?"

Swimmer 3: "Yawn. This pace is so easy. We must be swimming 2:00 per 100, if that."

Swimmer 4: "What are these guys doing? My heart rate is barely above resting."

As a coach it can be highly entertaining to watch and see these swimmers start to appreciate just how powerful and worthwhile drafting and pace lining can be. We often build sighting into these pace line exercises, too, to make it great race simulation practice. By sensibly practicing this with two to four athletes of similar speed you could even set up this type of pace line in a race with your friends.

Deck-Ups

Many Tower 26 athletes love to hate deck-ups, but I have been proud to include them in my workouts for years, even when people thought I was crazy to do so. Put simply, a deck-up is as follows: At the end of your interval, you touch the wall, climb out of the pool immediately, and get up onto the pool deck. You stand up, run for about 10 seconds, and then dive back into the water to begin your next repetition. If the pool where you train does not allow running on the pool deck, you can stand and jog on the spot. At the pool we use in Los Angeles, athletes exit the water, deck up, run around the bleachers (a 10–15-second jog), and then reenter the water. We incorporate a lot of deck-ups into training sessions during the open-water skill-building phase and the race-ready phase because they are a perfect simulation of the heart-rate spike you experience as you exit the water in the first transition, from swim to bike. During the swim section of a triathlon, you obviously spend the entire time in the horizontal position while in the water. When it comes

time to exit the water, you might experience a huge heart-rate spike and blood rush; in fact, some people feel light-headed or dizzy. Deck-ups prepare you for this feeling, and when repeated time and again in training, they will help you adapt to it. After a short period (typically three weeks) you find yourself performing deck-ups with relative ease, multiple times per workout. They also help you overcome the discomfort of transitioning from one sport to the next, even the bike to the run. Adapting to deck-ups in training is one of many key skills that help you to manage the race, rather than the race managing you. This is all part of becoming race ready.

During the open-water skill-building phase and the race-ready phase, we often include deck-ups as part of the warm-up or pre-main set. Examples might include an 800 yard/meter swim, all at easy effort, with a deck-up after every 100. We might also do sets of 4 × 50 meters, progressing effort, with a deck-up between each 50. As the racing season progresses, we build deck-ups into almost every main swim set.

Race Takeout Speed

Learning to swim at race takeout speed is a key skill for race day. Too many athletes fail to train at this intensity but attempt to start their race at this effort . . . and then wonder why they blow up shortly afterward. Training at this intensity will help you manage effort so that you are in control of your pace and your race. As with so many aspects of open-water racing, it is all about getting familiar with the discomfort involved. At Tower 26, we often swim 200-yard/meter repeats, where the first 50 meters are at race takeout speed (90 percent effort) and then the remaining 150 meters are about settling into race pace (at 80–85 percent effort). This is a lot easier said than done and requires practice, largely because the second 50 will still feel hard as a result of your heart rate being high from the first 50 at a higher intensity. You have to learn to settle into a more comfortable pace while adjusting to your heart rate coming down. A large part of this is learning to focus on stroke mechanics and cadence rate during that second 50. You cannot just switch off and start swimming at a much lower intensity. It is tough, but that is why we practice it regularly and expect you to grow accustomed to it.

OCEAN WORKOUTS

At our ocean workouts in Santa Monica, California, we swim once a week on Wednesday mornings after the water temperature has stayed consistently above 60 degrees Fahrenheit for two weeks. This typically means we begin ocean workouts in early May, and they run until late October or early November. I am well aware of many other triathletes who train in sub-60-degree water, but this is ill-advised. Coaches training triathletes in lower temperatures are exposing them to risks and increasing the likelihood of medical issues. We have a responsibility to protect athletes that is greater than financial gain and profit, and we should work to prevent or limit medical incidents from cold-water exposure.

After our ocean workouts begin, they become the key workout of the week for all Tower 26 athletes. Back in 1988, a few swimmers started doing these workouts, and now there are more than a couple hundred athletes of all abilities attending them every week. We split the group into four or five small groups based on speed, and each group tackles the same circuit but does so a different number of times, depending on fitness. For example, Group 1, our pro and elite age-groupers, might complete 6 to 10 circuits per session, whereas Group 5, our novices, would do 3 or 4 circuits. Over the years, we have had several hundred professional athletes join these workouts, some just visiting for a couple of weeks and others who became part of the program for years. They soon learn that the skills and experience they acquire from our ocean workouts and our pool sessions at this time of year enable them to approach race day anywhere in the world with the utmost confidence. In all likelihood they have already faced almost every type of situation or ocean element imaginable. The different conditions each week provide great physical and mental preparation for race day. Athletes start to learn that they can show up to the beach in Santa Monica on a Wednesday morning, and they might face tough conditions, or the ocean could look much like a lake—glassy, calm, and smooth. This alone is great practice for race day: learning to adapt, being versatile, and reacting to whatever conditions you encounter.

Low-Value Versus High-Value Open-Water Swimming

When new athletes join us, I often inquire about their previous training history and whether they have had open-water swim training. All too often I hear, "Oh, I just swim for forty minutes in the lake, but I never seem to improve." These steady-state, continuous swims, which seem so popular, might have some value for the first few occasions. A swim like this might involve one entry and one exit and involve some sighting practice. Depending on whether they swim with buddies, it might include some drafting or pace lining. So, during any given session, aside from the training value from the execution of the swim itself, there is limited race simulation or practice. This does not enhance open-water experience, and, although such swimmers might gain some confidence, it is diluted confidence. By contrast, in a typical ocean swim at Tower 26, you will practice—on multiple occasions—all or most of the following: sighting, drafting, pace lining, maneuvering in a pack, race takeout speed, changes in speed, turning around buoys, reading the surf, catching waves, dolphin diving, and race exits. This might be included in one circuit in as many as 20 sessions during the season. Add to this different conditions each week, and you can soon see how great a bank of experience you can build in a relatively short time.

Of course, you do not need to be on the beach at Tower 26 to reap these rewards; you can easily set up your own open-water training course. Ideally, find some training buddies who are all at a similar fitness level. As best you can, design a course that starts with a straight 100-meter stretch before you reach a turn (this can be a left or right turn, marked with a buoy, or just counting strokes). Swim another 200–300 meters parallel to shore before reaching another turn and then swimming 100 meters back to shore. Exit the water, and jog back to your start line. You are typically looking for a total of 8–10 minutes of swimming per loop. After you have a course set, then you can start adding in all of the race simulation skills. Very soon, you will be practicing all of the variables of open-water racing.

OPEN-WATER RACING TACTICS

You might think racing tactics are the preserve of the elites, but I think it is well worth athletes of all abilities to have at least some awareness of the dos and don'ts of open-water swimming tactics. Here are a few of my favorite rules:

Always warm up before the race starts

In my experience, approximately 90 percent of athletes do not warm up adequately. You cannot expect to start swimming at race takeout speed as soon as the gun goes off if your heart rate is only marginally above its resting rate. That kind of demand on the body necessitates a thorough warm-up that elevates core temperature and heart rate so that when the race starts, your body and mind are ready to go. Think about your best performances in workouts: Do they come at the very start, when you first dive in, or does it take you 30 minutes (or more) before you feel your body coming around? Getting your blood moving and your body adequately warmed up before the gun goes off can truly make or break your race experience. A warm-up does not need to be epic: a gentle 8- to 10-minute jog is ideal. Follow this up with an in-water warm-up, which you should practice in training so that it becomes second nature. We have a routine warm-up protocol every athlete learns and executes on race day, which you'll find in the open-water skill-building workouts at the end of the chapter.

Never get boxed in

There is no worse place to be than in the middle of the pack with people all around you. Although you'll be getting a draft, you'll also be experiencing a high amount of physical contact, and it will be far from comfortable. Ideally, when swimming in a pack, you always want to have at least one side open to you. Always try your best to position yourself in this way, but if you do find yourself stuck in the middle, then you have a couple of options available. By rolling over onto your back and taking one or two backstrokes, you should be able to maneuver yourself out of the boxed-in spot. However, this backstroke roll is by no means an easy move and should be rehearsed in training before you attempt it in a race. You could also stop and try to dive under the swimmers boxing you in so that you are then swimming on one side of the pack, but this could be a high-risk move if you end up getting spat out of the pack entirely. In elite racing, it is not uncommon to try to box in the best competitors. Countering a tactic like this is an advanced technical skill.

Be able to shake someone off your hip or your feet

We've outlined the benefits of drafting someone else, but what if you find someone drafting off of you? It can feel like they're slowing you down and dragging you backward, and you might not feel inclined to give someone a free ride around the swim course. Here's a handy trick I've learned that usually works well for ridding yourself of someone on your feet or hips: You will need to slow down slightly, so that they come up alongside you, and as they do so, you can start angling ever so slightly off course, perhaps by just 1 or 2 degrees to the right (if swimming toward a buoy on the left). After doing this, you make a very quick and sudden sharp surge back to the left, ideally taking them by surprise and opening up enough of a gap to drop them from your side and thereby lose the draft advantage. You do need to have some definite changes of speed available to execute this successfully, so again, this is something to practice in training if you want to nail it on race day.

Be able to change speeds

As outlined above, you need to be able to change speeds with relative ease if you want to fully maximize your open-water skills and tactics. This has to be built into training, and you need to be familiar with the discomfort of going from 90 percent effort to settling into 80–85 percent effort. Being able to do this is ideal not only at the start of a race but also if you find yourself in a pack scenario and want to use surges to see if you can lose some people. Quite often, these types of surges will help break up a big pack or blow swimmers off the back, especially in elite racing. Being well warmed up is critical to the execution of this.

Read the currents

When you are swimming in the ocean, there might be a strong current, and knowing how to assess the current gives you key information on where to start, which route to take toward the buoys, where to position yourself in a pack, and even what type of stroke to use. When you are swimming in a positive current (swimming with the current), then you can use a more elongated stroke. When swimming in a negative current (or, against it), then you will likely need to use a punchy stroke with higher tempo and faster cadence. If swimming with a lateral current (to one side or the other), then you could consider trying to position yourself with someone to that side to try to protect you from the current and chop (as cyclists do when riding in crosswinds). If you are unsure of the current, always ask a lifeguard or race director to help you assess it.

Always know the racecourse

It never ceases to amaze me when I see athletes standing on the start line looking out at the swim course and asking their competitors which way they are supposed to go. You have invested a significant amount of time, effort, and money into preparing for this race, so please do not fail to do your homework on something as basic as the course set-up. It takes no time at all to check out the race map online beforehand. Memorize its outline, how many buoys there are, what color they are, if turn buoys are a different color and/or different size compared with marker buoys, how many turns you will take, and what the distance is between turn buoys and marker buoys. As soon as you get to the race venue, take some time to check out the course, and if there is an opportunity to swim it prior to race day, then this is an absolute must. Look for landmarks you can use for sighting, and take note of where the sun is: Is there a stretch of the course where you will be swimming into the sun? Are there any tight turns or potential places of congestion (this typically occurs if you have a turn soon after the start line)? Do not just rely on people swimming in front of you; they could easily be taking you off course, and if you're on our training plan, they are not as prepared as you, so don't follow them.

ATHLETIC IQ

As you can probably tell from some of my racing tactics, open-water racing isn't just about learning a skill and practicing it. It takes some intelligence and smarts, too, to execute some of these skills well. I've coached many professional athletes who are excellent pool swimmers, but as soon as you put them in a dynamic environment such as the ocean, where they are faced with making split-second decisions, they find it difficult. Conversely, other athletes excel in dynamic conditions. I have found that athletes who have a background in racing fast-paced, strategic events do well in open-water swimming even if they have not come from a swimming background. Sean Jefferson is a perfect example of this. Sean is a sub-four-minute-mile runner who came to me in 2012 wanting to improve his swim in the hopes of making it onto the 2016 USA Olympic triathlon team. He could run as fast as anyone in the sport, but his swimming needed significant improvement if he were to unleash his potential in ITU racing. In one of the first ITU races he did after we began working together, he exited the water some four and a half minutes behind the front pack. Unlike in an Ironman, in ITU racing that is too much time. Sean worked hard in the pool and in open water, and over the period of a year he made huge gains. In another Olympic-distance race 12 months later, he had dropped four minutes from his time, exiting the water just 30 seconds behind the same lead swimmer from a year earlier and putting himself in contention. This was no fluke swim because he subsequently exited 70.3 races in less than 24 minutes, with the lead swimmers. Of course, a great deal of physical training was involved in this achievement, but Sean's high athletic IQ also played a significant role. Early in our time working together, I realized that an athlete highly competitive in such a strategic event—he ran a 3:56 mile and is a former NCAA mile champion—already possesses all the cunning and wile to excel in open-water racing. He already had a great deal of tactical awareness, so I knew I needed to import some of this from his running background and export some of my open-water strategy and knowledge, trying to ensure that at some point they intersected. They absolutely did, and Sean was always able to elevate his game in open water.

Cameron Wurf and Andrew Talansky, former professional cyclists turned Iron-man athletes, are two further examples of how this works. Road racing in cycling involves high-level strategy and tactical awareness. It is not always the fittest, fastest rider who wins but the smartest, most cunning, and least risk averse. I know athletes with this kind of background have the ability to absorb a lot of information and can make game-changing critical decisions in fractions of a second. They know how to execute similar moves on the bike, so it is a case of teaching them basic skills in the water, working on stroke mechanics and flaws, and then giving them as many opportunities as possible to execute these skills in training so they have a bank of swim-specific experience to take into racing. Of course, when swimming there is less information available to athletes than there might be while running on the track or riding on the road (that is, swimmers can see only what is just in front of them, unless sighting), so athletes switching sports do need to learn to have a higher awareness of what is happening in the pack, but this is something that comes from frequent sighting. In the space of a year, Wurf took 10 minutes off his Ironman swim split, going from posting 60-minute swims to 50-minute swims. With his cycling already a huge asset, taking this kind of time off his swim really helped catapult him to success.

RACE SIMULATION FOR THE POOL | Workout

This workout is perfect preparation for race day. It starts off with our race-day warm-up protocol, conditions permitting. If the weather is cold on race day (water temperature at 60 degrees Fahrenheit and below) execute a dry-land warm-up (8–10-minute jog), and then consider dunking your head in the water or splashing yourself with some water, but nothing else.

WARM-UP

5:00 easy swimming

5:00 as:
> 30 strokes easy, 30 strokes faster,
> 30 strokes easy, 25 strokes faster,
> 30 strokes easy, 20 strokes faster,
> 30 strokes easy, 15 strokes faster,
> 30 strokes easy, 10 strokes faster,
> 30 strokes easy, 5 strokes faster

Progressively increase the effort on each of the "faster" blocks and include sighting.

Take a brief rest, then repeat the 5:00 block in reverse:
> 30 strokes easy, 5 strokes faster,
> 30 strokes easy, 10 strokes faster
> until you reach 30 strokes easy, 30 strokes faster
> Ensure those 30 strokes faster are at race takeout speed.

If short on time, skip the last 5:00 block.

MAIN SET

Note: Times and distances shown below are for Level 1 advanced swimmers. Adjust accordingly based on fitness/speed.

3 × 50 fast at race takeout effort, 90% and above

Set a fixed interval, allowing 0:03–0:05 rest. Do the first 50 from a dive. After the third 50, go straight into the next effort.

300 at 85% effort, settling in to consistent, sustainable race pace

Heart rate will be high to start, following the fast 50s, so perceived effort will feel high, too. Learn to cope with that and settle in to a sustainable 85% effort.

50 at 90–95% effort

This is a final surge effort that mimics the surge you might need to make in a race to bridge up to a group ahead or try to drop swimmers from your pack. Make it hard and fast.

Repeat 2 to 3 rounds of this main set.

POOL SPEEDPLAY

WARM-UP

Stretch cords

6:00–7:00 of easy swimming followed by 600 as 25 kick/75 swim, no fins

Increase effort as you progress through the 600.

MAIN SET

4 × 10:00 swims, as follows:

1. Swim 10:00 at 75% effort
2. Swim 10:00 at upper aerobic effort, 80–85% effort
   Sight twice per 25, and deck up after each 100, then jog for 0:10 before diving back in.
3. 2 × 5:00 swims at 75–80% effort, taking 0:30 rest between each effort.
4. 5–8 × 100, taking about 0:45 rest between each 100.

   On set 4, the first 50 of each 100 should be at race takeout speed, with three sightings per lap.
   Drop intensity to 80–85% on the second 50, sighting twice per lap. Deck up at the end of each 100.

COOL DOWN

Recovery pull set

WARM-UP

Practice this race-simulation warm-up both in the pool and open water so that it becomes second nature on race day.

5:00 easy swimming

5:00 as:
> 30 strokes easy, 30 strokes faster,
> 30 strokes easy, 25 strokes faster,
> 30 strokes easy, 20 strokes faster,
> 30 strokes easy, 15 strokes faster,
> 30 strokes easy, 10 strokes faster,
> 30 strokes easy, 5 strokes faster

Increase the effort on each of the "faster" blocks, and include sighting, too.

After a brief rest, repeat the 5:00 block in reverse:
> 30 strokes easy, 5 strokes faster,
> 30 strokes easy, 10 strokes faster . . .
> until you reach 30 strokes easy, 30 strokes faster
> Ensure the final 30 strokes faster are at race takeout speed.

If you are short on time, just do one of the 5:00 blocks, not both.

After completing the warm-up, exit the water and return to the shoreline to begin the main set.

MAIN SET

Execute four full loops, as follows:

1. Starting on the shore, run into the water to simulate a race start. Swim fast to the first turn (~100 m), and then shut it down, bringing effort to 70% for the remainder of the loop. Exit the water and jog back to the start line. Take about 2:00 rest before starting the second loop.

2. Perform another race start, running into the water and swimming hard through the first turn all the way to the second buoy before bringing effort to 70%. Exit the water, and jog back to the start line. Again, take about 2:00 recovery.

3. This loop is all-out fast; 6–8 minutes of high output. Execute a race start from the shore, swim at race takeout speed with a high frequency of sightings, ideally every 6 strokes. Practice a smooth exit, running back to your start line. Recover for 2:00 to 3:00.

4. All recovery. Swim a final loop at recovery effort.

You can repeat this main set, but start all swims in the water so as to gain valuable practice at in-water race starts. Doing this twice through is an extremely tough and intense workout and can take up to 90 minutes. Prepare to feel tired after this!

This workout provides highly valuable race practice because each loop involves a race start, race takeout effort, sighting, practice turning around buoys, drafting, pack swimming (if swimming with others), and exits. As you could be doing up to eight loops, you can see how much experience and confidence it can help bring to your open-water swimming.

9

Race Preparation

YOU HAVE DONE ALL THE HARD WORK, and your race looms large on the horizon. Now all that stands between you and race day is your taper, a reduction in your training load as you prepare your body and mind to race. Much has been written and hypothesized about the dark art of tapering: Get it wrong, and you can arrive at the start line either too flat or too fatigued; get it right, and you will have one of those magical days where you achieve a PR and feel powerful. Many athletes (and coaches) can get the taper wrong as frequently as they get it right. It is not uncommon to see professional athletes on fire all season reach the start line at Kona and fail to impress—or even finish.

Getting your taper right can involve a lot of trial and error, and I'm not convinced many coaches can honestly say they have it 100 percent dialed in. After triathletes find what works for them, you will often see them repeating it, even down to what side of the bed they get out of on race morning and what color socks they wear. I think tapering is more of a psychological phenomenon than a physical one. Get your head right, and the rest will follow.

PLANNING YOUR TAPER

The type of taper you follow will change depending on the importance of the race. We encourage athletes to label races A, B, or C in terms of significance. C races are usually training races in which we are not looking for peak performance. You might be using the event as an opportunity to test something specific (bike position, fueling, etc.) or knock off the rust after a long period away from racing. There would be little to no taper for a C race. B races are more important, so we would look to scale training back slightly. If you are doing two A workouts a week, plus one B and one C session, this would usually mean you would do your first A session of the week in full but reduce the second A workout slightly.

An A race is an event at which you are looking for optimal performance. We want you firing on all cylinders from the moment the gun goes off. When tapering for an A race, you would usually scale back the intensity of both A workouts during race week, but you would still be looking for solid volume from your Tuesday workout, around 75 minutes of swimming. Your run mileage would have already been reduced, so you are looking to maintain some of this aerobic conditioning in the pool instead. It need not be complex or confusing: Ultimately, what we are looking to do with your taper is prepare your body and mind for optimal energy and performance come race day.

Athletes have a lot of questions about tapering: How much should I taper? When should I start cutting back my training? Will I get too tired if I don't rest more? How much intensity should I keep in my training? The questions hardly stop there, but I think this is partly because there are a lot of misconceptions when it comes to tapering for endurance events.

Reducing Volume

The traditional taper associated with elite pool swimming follows many months of higher-volume training and then a block of sprint work in the leadup to a key race. This often leaves a swimmer feeling terrible when heading into a two- to three-week taper period. During this time, training volume might be lowered, but intensity and race-specific pacing is still included. The body is bouncing back from the high-volume workload it has just undertaken. We have traditionally seen this type of taper migrate into triathlon, but applying the same taper methodology to sports so distinctly different seems potentially fraught with risks.

Of course, the distance you are racing will inform how you plan your taper, but for an endurance athlete racing a 70.3 distance or shorter, this traditional two- to three-week taper is a surefire recipe for disaster. In that short period, you can become flat and stagnant and lose some of the sharpness you have banked ahead of your race. Instead, you would be better off taking a couple of reduced-volume weeks four weeks out from your race, and then go into the final two-week block feeling rested and refreshed. Use those first two to three days of race week to hit some higher intensity work and really get your engine firing on all cylinders. When you are 48 hours out from the race, then it's time to rest. Stay active, keep moving your body, perhaps take one day of complete rest where you stay off your feet as much as possible, and except for a few shorter, faster intervals in the pool, keep all other swimming at active recovery effort.

Managing Fatigue and Frequency

The question of how much to reduce your training is tough. Primarily, it depends on the type of athlete you are and your typical training load. If you are a time-crunched age-grouper swimming only 3,000 meters twice a week, then there is no need for you to taper. Your frequency and volume of training is not high enough to warrant it. I would urge you to maintain your standard swimming. Conversely, if we have a professional athlete swimming six or seven times a week, then we would look to cut back volume and intensity, but we would likely still keep frequency of sessions quite high (at least five swims in race week). It is vital not to lose your feel for the water, and this could happen if you dramatically dropped from seven swims to two, for example. It could also depend on whether this athlete has a swimming background, along with factors such as age and racing experience. No athlete responds in the same way when it comes to tapering and preparing to race.

Tower 26 athletes swimming frequently (three or more times a week) experience a slight reduction in their weekly volume and certainly in the intensity of their training, too, but the frequency of sessions stays similar. In many ways, the periodization of our multiphase yearly program ensures that athletes arrive at their A races sharp, yet well rested. The bulk of the higher-volume work has been done during the build phase, from January to April. When we enter the ensuing open-water skill-building phase, there is an automatic drop in volume and an increase in intensity. We don't reduce the volume too much, but the intensity rises and stays high into the next phase, the race-ready phase. This phase, from June through October, is specific to the demands of racing. In race week, it means we are practicing warm-ups, deck-ups, and plenty of race-pace endurance work at 80–85 percent effort. There is some higher-intensity work, but not too much—enough to spark your engine, but not fatigue it. We want to keep skill building, endurance, and speed all on tap.

As a triathlete looking to optimize your taper, I think it is imperative to understand just how corrosive running is on the body. It builds fatigue fast. You do not want to lose too much endurance, so a good alternative is to run less but not reduce swimming. This allows you to still train your aerobic system and not lose any conditioning while minimizing the higher impact of running. Scaling back your running 10–14 days out from your race and replacing some of it with swimming is highly recommended.

The biggest mistake you can make when tapering is to equate your taper with complete rest. This is certainly not the case. If your body is used to training for 10–15 hours a week, and on race week you do little else than sit on the couch, you will not be raring to go come race morning. You will likely feel groggy and sloth-like—quite the opposite of how we want you to feel! Keeping some higher-intensity work in your training during race week is hugely important. I would encourage you to include high-intensity work in your swim sessions up until two to three days out from your race, and then plan a restful 48 hours leading into the event.

Sleep, nutrition, stress, and travel are also contributing factors to the success of your race week and ultimately your race. If you can control as many of these factors as possible, you are setting yourself up for success and your best performance. The reduction in training volume in the weeks leading into your race offers an ideal opportunity to try to increase sleep. Even an extra 30–60 minutes a night could have a positive impact.

PLAN A SUCCESSFUL TAPER | Keys

- ▶ If you usually swim two or three times a week, don't start swimming five or six times during race week.
- ▶ Replace some runs with swims in the 10–14 days prior to the race.
- ▶ If you miss a session, don't try to play catch up and cram too much into race week.
- ▶ Don't try to get fitter in race week. It won't work.
- ▶ Don't neglect mental preparation. What goes on between your ears during race week is probably more important than anything else.

Sharpening Your Mental Game

In my experience, whether you are coming off of the best or worst training block of your life, it does not matter as much as your mental state. If your head is in the right place going into a race, even if training in recent weeks was less than ideal, the odds of you succeeding and having a great race are significantly higher. Belief matters when it comes to racing. I often hear the most successful athletes say: "I made up my mind that I could do it—and I did." It is no surprise that these athletes also tend to be hugely successful in other aspects of their lives. The mind controls the body. Of course, we have to take care of physiology, but ensuring your head is in the right place is key.

I share an anecdote with scores of athletes season after season to illustrate how self-talk impacts success. Put simply, we each possess a good wolf and a bad wolf.

Positive self-talk, mantras, and visualization will feed the good wolf. Doubts, anxiety, and negative self-talk will fuel the bad wolf. The wolf you choose to feed will play a role in the outcome of your race as well as your enjoyment of it. The same could be said for your work and family life, relationships—in fact, just about everything! During a taper we typically have a lot more time available. Many athletes fall into the trap of using the time they usually spend training to worry about or overthink their race. The thoughts creep in: "I haven't done enough training," "I'm not as fit as last year," "I'm going to struggle in the swim," or "Injuries have hindered my training lately." Given enough airtime, these thoughts will soon multiply. They can be crippling. I have seen professional athletes in the shape of their lives get bogged down in negative, critical, ruminative thinking. And some of us are predisposed to think this way, making the threat of the bad wolf even more ominous. As a coach, the best thing I can do to pull athletes out of this spiral of negative thinking is to remind them they have a choice of which wolf they feed.

I ask them to think about their best workouts and visualize themselves executing a brilliant race. Part of this visualization involves planning to remain extremely process driven throughout the entire event. It comes back to being mindful and staying in the moment. Even a 12-hour Ironman race can be broken down minute by minute. There is so much to do and focus on, even in the swim alone: executing your best swim start, drafting, sighting, approaching turn buoys, monitoring effort, exiting the water, and removing your wet suit as you reach transition. If you can remain fully focused on yourself as you do each of these things, then you stand a great chance of remaining process driven throughout your event, which significantly improves your chances of success. Focusing solely on outcomes and objectives—such as split times and position—is less conducive to optimal performance, especially when something unfavorable happens, as it almost always does during a long-distance triathlon. Be prepared for all eventualities. The bad wolf will raise his ugly head, especially when something does not go to plan; if you have positive thoughts waiting in the wings, you will be in a good position. I tell my athletes never to give the bad wolf more than three seconds of airtime. Any more time than that, and it's all too easy to succumb to the negative tales of woe. Do not feed him! Put him back in his place by bringing in the good wolf. Remember, though, that this is a skill like any other and needs practice, which is why it is so important to use your workouts as opportunities not just to get physically fitter but mentally stronger, too.

MENTAL REHEARSAL IN TRAINING

If you are going to be mentally prepared for racing, then mental rehearsal must have a regular place in your training. You cannot just show up on race day and expect everything to flow seamlessly. It requires mental practice and attention if you wish to see improvement. Visualize your race setting. Practice focusing on yourself. Get into the right headspace, and think about what you need to execute your best race.

Have some mantras lined up and ready to use on race day. Prepare by using them in your training day after day. Here are two of my favorites from my own racing career, from one of my coaches and my dad, respectively. My coach would say, "It only hurts to win until you win." The exhilaration of crossing the finish line or winning truly anesthetizes the pain. My dad would tell me, "If you are hurting, the guy next to you is hurting just as much—otherwise he'd be ahead of you." This would help me handle the psychology of racing, especially when it became all too easy to assume others weren't suffering in the way I was. I used these mantras not only during races but also before races because they would help me prepare my mind for when moments of doubt, fatigue, or suffering really took hold. The bad wolf will undoubtedly pop up at the most inopportune times, so know how to banish him and bring the good wolf to the fore. Find something specific to you. Sometimes your mantra is born out of a particularly intense training session or block. Above all else, it is a reminder to believe that you have what it takes to execute the race for which you have trained.

To help with mental rehearsal, I deliberately design Saturday workouts, our B sessions, with a significant amount of race takeout speed and race-pace swimming. I like to do this on a Saturday because so many races are held on the weekend, so the practice helps build that mental familiarity. Knowing what to expect on race day—as well as what to do—is half of the battle and a key part of your preparation. It comes back to the three Fs once again: we want familiarity, which we achieve through frequency, because we want to avoid fear. Almost everyone will have nerves on race day—that is to be expected—but I also want athletes to feel an underlying sense of confidence: in their training, in their preparation, and in their knowledge. I want athletes to be standing on the start line thinking: "I am ready. No one else in the world has done the training I've done. No one else is more prepared than I am."

Preparing for the Swim

There's an added dimension to being mentally prepared for the swim I think few athletes fully consider. The swim is almost always the first part of your race, except in some pool triathlons. It is also where people experience the greatest anxiety, either in anticipation of the race start or the challenges of open water. It can very easily open the door for the bad wolf to creep in and get a hold of you. If you have not done sufficient mental preparation, negative thinking can set in on the swim and contaminate your entire race. I have heard far too many athletes say, "I got punched in the swim, I lost focus, and then I couldn't stop thinking about it for the rest of the race." They might go on to tell me they'd been feeling great while cycling or running, but they let that one negative event pollute the entire race.

When athletes look at their watches upon exiting the swim, the same self-sabotage can ensue. They might have been hoping to post a specific swim split, but on seeing their time, they discover that they have swum slower, perhaps much slower, than they hoped. This disappointment rattles them—they stop focusing on the task at hand and become consumed by this perceived "failure." This just shows the dangers of relying too heavily on outcomes and data-oriented feedback rather than being process driven. If athletes look at their watches and see times they don't like, they need to remember that a range of factors could be affecting the data. Perhaps the course is slightly long; perhaps conditions are tough. There are many details to consider, but none of them need be analyzed or debated mid-race.

If you are going to look at your watch as you exit the water, be mindful that the data might not be entirely reliable. Never let your time shape your mindset for the remainder of the race. And even if something detrimental happens during the swim, part of the challenge of competition is to bounce back, both mentally and physically. If you are well prepared mentally as well as physically, then you will have all the necessary tools in your toolbox to cope with all eventualities.

At the elite level, resilience is what separates the very best athletes from all of the other great athletes. It is an incredibly important component of optimal performance. As a coach, I want to help you have the most positive experience on race day. At Ironman events especially, it is common to see people walking along the run course with their heads hanging low and their body language screaming defeat and failure. This is not enjoyable; this is not why you've spent thousands of dollars and hundreds of hours preparing. It is important to me to make sure any athlete with whom I'm working has every chance not only of success but also of enjoying their race experience, too. There are no shortcuts or magic bullets. Practice becoming a resilient racer, and you will walk away from every competition with a smile and a great deal of satisfaction.

The Importance of Warming Up

Making every aspect of your race day as routine as possible is key to success, and your warm-up certainly should not be an exception to this rule. A thorough warm-up is essential for optimal performance. Unfortunately, not enough triathletes have realized this. I have been coaching triathletes since 1983, and ever since then I have looked on with equal parts dismay and disbelief as I see about 90 percent of them fail to execute a warm-up, which means about 90 percent of them are failing to set themselves up for optimal success. Your race-day warm-up routine should be built into your training and practiced time and again so that it becomes learned, familiar, and second nature. At Tower 26, we practice our standard race warm-up routine every single Saturday in race season. Here is the full 15–20-minute version, but it can be pared back as needed:

OPEN-WATER WARM-UP | Protocol

Warm up with 5:00 easy swimming, then swim:
  30 strokes easy, 30 strokes faster;
  30 strokes easy, 25 strokes faster;
  30 strokes easy, 20 strokes faster;
  30 strokes easy, 15 strokes faster;
  30 strokes easy, 10 strokes faster;
  30 strokes easy, 5 strokes faster

This should take about 5 minutes. Each time increase the effort on the faster strokes so that those final five strokes are close to 90% effort.

If tired, take a short rest and then repeat the pattern in reverse (i.e., 30 strokes easy, 5 strokes faster; 30 strokes easy, 10 strokes faster), finishing with 30 strokes easy, 30 strokes faster where those final 30 strokes are at takeout speed.

This is perfect preparation for the gun going off. Ideally, try to swim these from the swim start line and practice sighting the buoys on course for the first few hundred meters so that there are no surprises.

The importance of having an established warm-up protocol ahead of race day cannot be overstated. Mark Spitz conducted the same warm-up before every race of his career. Based on how he felt during his warm-up, he knew whether it was going to be a good day or a more painful one.

Race-day morning can be hectic, especially when you factor in all of the logistics involved in triathlon racing and the inevitable nerves. Budget your time carefully so that you are able to execute your warm-up. Unfortunately, many race directors do not share my view on the importance of a swim warm-up, and sometimes even the pro athletes have limited time before the gun goes off. Be prepared for this and plan accordingly, even if it means finding a nearby pool to warm up in. If athletes I coach come to me after the race and tell me they weren't able to warm up, I don't want to hear it. You've done months of hard work and preparation for this race; don't fail yourself now with something as simple as a warm-up venue. Don't come to me with the problem; just find the solution—your warm-up is that vital. To prove this to my swimmers, I will "surprise" them once or twice a season. They show up on the pool deck expecting me to prescribe a full warm-up, but in fact I tell them they will be swimming a 20-minute race-effort time trial as soon as we get in the water. I give them three to five minutes, and they can use this time to mentally prepare or get ready on dry land with stretch cords or a light jog. It is always fascinating to see how different athletes ready themselves for this swim.

There can and will be occasions when the water temperature is too cold to warrant an in-water warm-up. In this case, always warm up on dry land with an 8–10-minute easy jog, and prior to the race start, dunk your entire head several times in the water to familiarize yourself with the temperature and minimize the "brain freeze" cold water can induce. I believe there should be strict water-temperature rules in place for all races, not just the guidelines we presently have. There are dangers to swimming in extremely cold (or hot) water. We need to have stringent temperature parameters that help keep athletes safe, and it has always been my suggestion that these should be enforced so that no competition can take place if the water temperature is beneath 56 degrees Fahrenheit or above 84 degrees Fahrenheit. Race directors and governing bodies need to listen to the people who have the experience of the perils of swimming in these conditions. I never have—and likely never will—hold an open-water workout if the water is below 60 degrees Fahrenheit. The consequences of swimming in extremely cold or hot water can be fatal.

Equipment

When it comes to equipment for the swim, I always advise having at least two pairs of goggles with you: one clear, one tinted, so you have options for all weather conditions. Also, your wet suit can really play a critical role in your swim performance. Finding the right wet suit for you is not always an easy feat. There are now so many on the market, each tempting you with the promise of faster swim splits and maximum comfort. Believe none of it until you have tried it on and swum in it. Every athlete is different, and what works for one person can feel terrible for another. It is impossible to know how a suit will feel in the water until you've swum in it, and committing to buying one without having this data can be daunting and costly. For this reason, I advise athletes to do as much research as they can, talk to their training buddies, and ideally try borrowing one or two from similarly sized friends before committing to buying one. Use the Wet Suit Testing Protocol to find the best fit for you.

After you have purchased a suit, swim in it several times before your race, and make sure you swim for a duration similar to that of your event. This will help you get an idea of how it feels wearing it for that long, especially around the critical parts of your body such as your chest, arms, shoulders, and neck. It is not uncommon to find that the suit feels too tight around your chest and neck, which can prove problematic, especially at the swim start, when you might already feel anxious and have a higher breathing rate. A suit restricting your breathing too much will only worsen these feelings. This is why doing a few swims in your suit is so important because the suit will give a little as you continue to use it. In short, don't panic if the neck or chest feels too tight upon first use. If it still feels like this after several wears, then reconsider your sizing model. Remember, too, that each wet suit brand has a few different models of suit within its range: typically a cheaper entry-point suit, a mid-range suit, and a top-end expensive suit. They can vary in price from $200 to north of $1,200. We usually see stiffer, lower-quality neoprene in the less-expensive suits, which can actually be more beneficial for slower swimmers. Do not blindly assume that the most expensive suit is going to be the best for you—and certainly don't just opt for what looks good, what your training buddies choose to wear, or what you can get the best discount on.

It is always important to assess how your wet suit feels around your arms and shoulders. Wet suits are made of neoprene that under current race regulations is allowed to be up to 5 mm thick. Manufacturers typically make suits thicker around the hips to aid buoyancy and thinner around the arms and shoulders to minimize upper-body restriction. You want the material to be as thin and stretchy as possible around the shoulders and under the armpits. If you have limited mobility in your arms and shoulders for the duration of an Ironman swim, this could have a huge

WET SUIT TESTING

Performance can vary greatly from one wet suit brand or style to another, and of course, fit is highly individual. Before committing to a wet suit, you will need to test as many different brands as possible, ideally five or six if you can get access to that many. Borrowing different wet suits from friends who wear a similar size is a good strategy. Test no more than two or three wet suits at one time so that fatigue doesn't affect your results. You will need a friend or coach to help you because it's a blind test, meaning the swimmer cannot have access to the data or times until the protocol has been completed:

First, complete a thorough warm-up. Then put on the first wet suit and swim as follows:

5 × 100 at race-pace effort; 0:10–0:15 rest between efforts

Have your friend or coach record the time for each 100, along with your stroke rate and number of strokes per length. I recommend discarding the time for the first 100, which is often a little faster, and using the average time of the remaining four swims. Note: Your stroke rate refers to the number of strokes you are taking in a minute (strokes per minute, or spm), which is different from the number of strokes per length. For example, a Level 1 swimmer might have a stroke rate of 70 spm and take 14–16 strokes per 25 yards/meters.

Repeat the testing protocol with the second (and third) wet suit.

You will likely be surprised at the difference in performance from one suit to the next. The biggest time margin I've witnessed is 12 seconds per 100 yards/meters, which could make a difference of almost 8 minutes over the course of an Ironman swim. That's huge! I know how hard athletes train to take that margin of time off of their Ironman swim split, so this just shows how critical it is to find the right wet suit for you. It is well worth your time to do thorough research and get the most from your equipment.

impact on performance. On average, most swimmers execute more than 4,000 strokes during the course of an Ironman swim!

I encourage all athletes to test their wet suits at least once before their race. If you can only test it in the pool, that's fine, but if you have an opportunity to test it in open water, that's ideal. Testing it just once is better than not testing it at all. Emergency advice: If you're absolutely stuck and you're about to race in a wet suit you've never worn before, at least soak it in the bath the night before your race, which should help to loosen it slightly.

At the 1972 Olympic Games **MARK SPITZ** won seven gold medals with seven world records, an accomplishment that has yet to be repeated. Michael Phelps won more medals, but not all of them came via world-record times. Mark came on our *Be Race Ready* podcast to talk about the mental battle that nearly interrupted his 1972 Olympic feat. He was five races into those Games, and his sixth race was the 100-meter freestyle, the marquee event in swimming. He had taken a day of rest ahead of that sixth race, during which he had nothing to do except relax and prepare. He tweaked his back during the course of the day, and despite having a lot of physical therapy done, it seemed to trigger something in him, and he could not escape the doubts in his own head. He began thinking it would be better to scratch from the 100-meter freestyle, in part because he did not want to jeopardize his unblemished record so far at that Games. For at least 20 hours of that day leading up to his race, he was convinced that he should not compete—further proof that even the very best in the world can succumb to negative thinking.

Spitz eventually came to see his strengths and moved away from the ruminative, negative thinking that had led him to consider not competing. For him, the turning point was the realization that he owed it to himself to compete in the race. That is the hallmark of a champion. The question is not whether the mental blows will happen, but how you recover when they do.

His advice to athletes who find themselves at the mercy of the bad wolf was stark yet simple: "You have to get ahold of yourself. You need to take yourself back to a workout that was awesome. Wipe out all the negative thoughts and go back to a time when you felt phenomenal." Of course, Mark had a tremendous advantage over other swimmers given his phenomenal winning streak going into that race. He had already won five consecutive races with five world records at those Games. The margins of his victories in those events were some of the largest in swimming history.

As we now know, he did compete in the 100-meter freestyle at the 1972 Olympics—and won in the world record time of 51.22. I enjoy telling this story to triathletes of all ages and abilities to help them see that we can all get caught up in our thoughts at times, no matter our talent, speed, or name, but we can all find ways to learn to adapt and respond.

10

Athlete Development

WHATEVER YOUR AGE, ABILITY, OR GOALS, after a season of racing there's no doubt about it: You need to take a break. Many names are given to this period at the end of the racing year. Traditionally it was referred to as the off-season, but some coaches prefer to call it the postseason because, theoretically, we never want athletes to be 100 percent "off." Regardless of what you call it, though, there is no doubt in my mind that if you are looking for long-term success and longevity in endurance sports, then you need to wrap up each season with a dedicated period of relaxation and rejuvenation. It is essential for the physical, mental, and emotional well-being of every athlete, and none can consider themselves an exception to this rule. The triathlon racing season, especially now, is long, and it is currently possible to race year-round if you so desire. In my view, this is a dangerous endeavor because everyone needs some downtime. I typically recommend athletes race from April to September or October, but increasingly we are seeing people (professionals and age-groupers alike) keep their foot on the racing gas for an entire 12-month period. Ultimately, I believe this is detrimental, and such triathletes will, at some stage, experience a slump in fitness, motivation, or even health if they continue to chase peak performance for this long. And at a minimum they'll likely experience fractured relationships with family, close friends, and even coworkers as a result of their athletic imbalance.

After a heavy period of training, preparation for racing, and the race season itself, your body and mind need a break from this type of structure and regimen. We think about our muscular and skeletal systems needing a break, which, of course, they do. The mental and emotional period of rest and relaxation is equally important. There is always a considerable buildup to each and every A race. You invest so much of yourself into training and racing that after the season is complete, it is extremely important to take time to reboot and replenish all energy systems if you wish to fully recover. I say this assuming that athletes want longevity and sustained improvement over a number of years because, for me at least, this is the only way I work. Barely pausing to take a break before jumping into the next season is not sustainable—mentally or physically—and will lead to performance plateaus, burnout, or injury. If you are truly invested in enjoying your training and getting the most from your racing, then plan to take at least a month off from structured training at the end of your season. Many people take six to eight weeks and only return to a training schedule when they naturally feel their motivation and energy return. During this period, I like to advise athletes to invest in their family and friends, whom they might have neglected throughout the season. Now is the time to give back to them and find a way to thank them for all the support and love they've given you over the course of the year.

STRUCTURING THE POSTSEASON

How you structure your postseason is largely dependent on your strengths and weaknesses, along with your level of fatigue at the end of the season. The duration of your break might vary from year to year based on that year's training load, how you've been feeling and performing, any injuries you've sustained, returning time you've extracted from family, and what your goals are for the following year. Athletes are often fearful of taking a break because they are scared to lose the fitness they have worked so hard to gain. Although I can understand this rudimentary concept, it should not prevent you from stepping back and resting. You will lose some fitness, but really all you lose is the top-end speed and conditioning. Your aerobic base will remain, especially for those in the sport for a long time. You will not forget how to run, ride, or swim: You don't lose the muscle memory. Your body has a way of remembering what it can do. You will lose some muscular endurance, and you will feel fatigued a little faster when you first return to structured training, but there's a reason we want that to happen. By taking a break and resting the body and mind, we can then build back up the following year and achieve even greater levels of fitness, speed, strength, and power. That becomes incredibly hard to do if you carry on training from one year to the next without taking time off.

For those who come from a running background and are newer to swimming, it is a great opportunity to cut back on run mileage and focus instead on stroke mechanics and making some improvements in technique. Regardless of your background—because running is the most corrosive to your body and this time of year is geared toward recovery—I often recommend dropping run volume in favor of more time in the water. Swimming is far more restorative for the body. It helps promote recovery while still maintaining some aerobic conditioning and allows for a more developed technical foundation to absorb training load in the upcoming year.

For athletes used to working out once or more a day, it can be extremely hard to take time off. Staying active is okay—in fact, it's highly recommended—but do so with a focus on exercising, not training. Our bodies are used to moving every day, so if we suddenly stop doing that, it can create more problems than it solves, especially for our mental health. Move your body, but do so in such a way that the focus is on restorative activity. Make it as group oriented and sociable as possible. Do not wear a watch or look at any kind of data. This is not a time for GPS watches, bike computers, and heart rate monitors. Use this as an opportunity to try other sports you might not have done before or had limited time and energy to do during the race season, such as trail running, mountain biking, or skiing.

RETURNING TO TRAINING

When you do return to training, this is the perfect time of year to dedicate to improving your technique and mechanics. October through December is our technical phase, with a focus on stroke mechanics and drills, the majority of which are done at a low intensity. With zero impact on the body, swimming helps with this period of physical rejuvenation, and with a limited amount of higher-intensity workload, it also helps give the brain a break from the pressure and stimulation these workouts bring. This time of year is the ideal time to hire a coach to help you improve your mechanics and technique, but be sure to do your research on whom you hire. Do not waste this time of potential growth and development by doing endless drills. Make sure you are doing drills that have clear purpose and focus and are progressive in sophistication. Always follow them up with full swimming.

When looking for a coach, ideally try to find someone with triathlon swimming experience. That said, being with a coach who lacks this experience might still be better than being without a coach at all. Surround yourself with people who bring out the best in you and help you swim better and faster, and you will have no choice but to raise your game. One of the greatest things about triathlon is how warm and welcoming the community is. If you are a novice, be sure to tap into the wisdom and expertise of others because more experienced athletes often love to share their knowledge. As a newcomer to the sport, the very worst thing you can do is try to be an expert in something you're not. Don't try to fake it until you make it—because you won't! Hire a coach, join a team, and consult with those who do have the necessary expertise and experience. If you are interested in joining the Tower 26 program, this is the perfect time to do so because you will get a thorough base of technical work before the build phase starts in early January.

Athletes new to triathlon who jump straight into Ironman events are those I always want to mentor, telling them there's no rush. I always advise novices to start with a local sprint event, see if they like it, get a taste of the sport, and in due course progress to an Olympic-distance race. If they enjoy it, perhaps after a year or so they step up to racing a half-Ironman, and a couple of years after that they make the jump to Ironman events. The progression should be careful and well considered, at least if an athlete is looking to be involved in triathlon for a long time to come.

ATHLETE-COACH COLLABORATION

I have seen differing levels of collaboration between triathletes and coaches, which can be dependent on their experience and their swimming background. This can range from the coach being 100 percent in charge and the triathlete having zero input to a 50:50 relationship. If I'm working with professional triathletes who grew up as competitive swimmers and have a strong sense of the training stimulus to which they respond well, then I typically feel confident in trusting their input and feedback. When coaching a less experienced swimmer, I will take the reins more firmly: I am the teacher, they are the student, and it is not an equal professional relationship. This is not to say that this won't change in time as they gain more experience and develop as swimmers, but early on they must understand that I am guiding them and that I have the benefit of years of experience, which they lack. Coach-athlete relationships can be tricky and require communication, trust, and respect if they are to work well. I have seen many coaches "make" athletes, that is, take their raw talent and develop them into world-class professionals. This is the sign of a great coach. This caliber of coach is typically open to working collaboratively with other coaches, too, to build the best team and support network for triathletes. Coach Matt Dixon is a good example. Those who aren't open to networking are often inexperienced and have false confidence in their abilities. It is sometimes—not always—the case that triathletes "make" coaches, by which I mean one athlete's success catapults a coach to fame. Kudos is really only deserved if the coach can duplicate the success with another triathlete and another after that.

There can often come a time in any coach-athlete relationship when it is clear (to one party or both) that the triathlete should move on. Triathletes can reach a stage where they need a different stimulus, a new environment, or an alternative approach. This is simply part of professional sport. Whether I am working with an age-grouper or a professional, I never lose sight of the role I play in the triathlete's life, and I always respect that; I will not undervalue it or overstate it. As far as I'm concerned, the coach's duty does not change: You get to know the person before you can truly train the athlete, and then you can help develop a competitor ready to perform and excel in their sport. My responsibility as a coach always has been—and always will be—to set the tone, attitude, and style of the squad or team I am leading and to help every one of those athletes become their very best. Through our work together, you will learn more about yourself than you thought possible and achieve goals you previously thought unreachable. It is an honor, a privilege, and a blessing to be able to play a part in helping so many people realize their sporting dreams.

BALANCE AND REWARD IN SPORT

When novices join Tower 26, I know they will probably need two to three years in the program before we really see them acquiring the skills and fitness required to fulfill their potential. The athletes I've seen put in the work day after day, month after month, year after year, with patience, commitment, and consistency, are the ones who reap the greatest benefits. It means buying into the process and accepting that it can be a long and winding road. I enjoy helping athletes reach their goals over a period of years, yet I realize this approach is not for everyone. Those looking to build triathlon into their lifestyle and those willing to work consistently over the longer term are typically those who thrive athletically.

Many athletes underestimate the physical, mental, and emotional toll triathlon training and racing can take. Pausing at the end of each season not only to reflect and review but also to switch off and reboot is highly recommended for those looking to achieve long-term success. One of the best things about triathlon is how addictive it can be, but this can also be one of its biggest pitfalls. I have seen it become all-consuming, for amateur athletes especially. The sport should have its place in your life alongside work and family commitments, but it should rarely be the sole focal point. Triathlon tends to attract Type A personalities who are very much "all-or-nothing" people. As a coach, I like to help athletes learn the art of balance, which can be as instrumental in their success as guiding them with physical training. It is a double-edged sword because the personality types who thrive in this sport aren't afraid of hard work and sacrifice. I have found this particularly pernicious when it comes to novices training for their first 70.3 or full Ironman. They can quickly become overtrained, and they reach the start line of their race feeling mentally and physically burned out. Be careful in your approach to training and racing. Never let it take over your life, and only trust experienced, knowledgeable coaches to guide your program. Above all else, keep the sport in perspective.

After more than three decades of coaching triathlon, I have found that athletes can become what they feed. If you are self-obsessed and focused only on your training, you will ultimately limit the amount of enjoyment you gain from this sport. Invest time in those who love and support you and try to take a holistic approach to your training. See it as one part of your life, not the only part. Triathlon is a sport that can reward those willing to go the extra mile. It can be an endless pursuit, but that doesn't mean it should be your endless pursuit at the cost of all else. The impact of doing it too much, of not taking a break, and of not seeking a balanced lifestyle, can be far-reaching. I have seen age-group athletes go through divorce, lose their jobs, and suffer ill health when their obsession with triathlon overrides everything else.

Attorney **CHRIS WRIGHT** has reaped the benefits of consistent hard work and focused, race-specific training over a number of years. Chris is a busy father of three who runs his own law practice and has many commitments outside of triathlon. When he started our program in 2012, he was a 35- or 36-minute 70.3 swimmer. He committed to swimming two or three times a week, sometimes four if his schedule allowed, and he consistently chipped away, always learning and working hard. Even though he had a relatively small time budget each week, he committed completely to each workout he attended. His greatest strength might be the extent to which he is able to be present: He has a laser-like focus for whatever is in front of him and executes everything with an incredible amount of intention. Over the space of six to seven years, Chris has taken almost eight minutes off his 70.3 swim time, impressive for a man in his 50s without a swim or athletic background. His slow yet steady progression is a great example of the longer-term development on which I want you to set your sights.

EQUIPMENT

Triathletes are renowned for their love of gizmos, gadgets, and equipment. When it comes to swimming, I have found some items essential—many of these items help improve and refine core elements of technique, and others aid recovery and feel for the water. I have no endorsement agreements with any of the brands mentioned here. I take pride in testing a wide variety of equipment with zero incentive for doing so other than finding the best tools for triathletes. All of these items are available from Tower 26 (theswimmall.com) and are vital additions to your swim bag. In no order of preference or priority, outlined below are my must-have items.

Front-Mounted Snorkel

Excessive movement of the head is often the biggest cause of problems with stroke mechanics and technique, so we use the snorkel to help keep the head stationary. While you are wearing a snorkel, you have no reason to turn your head to breathe, which enables you to focus entirely on your stroke. We stick with our head mantra: no lifting, no tilting, no tucking; just a fixed, neutral head position with the water line at the center-top of the head when in the horizontal swim position. Keeping your head still is the most important reason to use a snorkel. It enables you to break down the stroke into bite-sized pieces and just focus on single elements. The primary focus while wearing a snorkel is alignment, where most issues with stroke

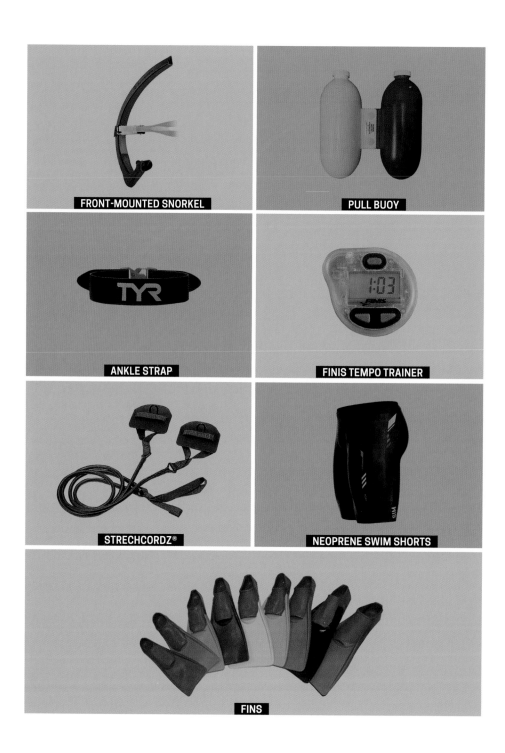

FRONT-MOUNTED SNORKEL

PULL BUOY

ANKLE STRAP

FINIS TEMPO TRAINER

STRECHCORDZ®

NEOPRENE SWIM SHORTS

FINS

mechanics occur. When keeping the head absolutely still, you can focus entirely on the alignment of your head, chest, hips, butt, and feet.

Pull Buoy

It is rare to meet triathletes who don't share a special bond with their pull buoys, without a doubt the favorite tool in their swim bags. The buoy lifts your body position in the water, creating less drag and enabling you to swim with greater ease and speed. It also helps subsidize body weight and lifts the legs, which in many triathletes are heavy from bike and run training. For men in particular, dense muscle mass in the quadriceps and hamstrings often creates drag that a pull buoy helps reduce. We always use the buoy along with a snorkel and ankle strap. These three items are essential for pulling. Together they enable us to work on creating a perfectly straight line that runs from your head to your toes, through your sternum, belly button, hips, knees, and ankles.

The Eney Buoy, a two-chamber buoy designed by Eney Jones of Boulder, Colorado, is larger than the standard-sized buoy, and each chamber has a cap that can be removed and the chamber filled with water. When the chambers are empty, the buoy mimics the buoyancy granted by a wet suit, so it is great for race simulation. When filled with water, it is heavy and will weigh the swimmer down, which makes it the perfect tool for some strength and power training. An example set maximizing the use of the Eney Buoy might look like this:

6 × 200 with the first 2 × 200 empty buoy chambers;
next 2 × 200 one chamber filled; next 2 × 200 both chambers filled

Swimming with a full buoy requires a higher stroke rate and a great deal of tautness, power, and strength. As water is removed from the chambers, swimming becomes easier, and swimmers are rewarded not only with what feels like "free speed" but also with a technical reminder of the importance of holding their body taut and aligned.

Buoys are essential tools on recovery days, typically Mondays. For many amateur triathletes, the bulk of their riding and running miles are done on the weekends, thus calling for Monday recovery. During our technical phase, especially when working on alignment, we rely heavily on buoys. They are also integrated into hard training sets in our build phase as a "wrapper"; that is, they come before and after higher intensity work. They are used to start the set with proper swim mechanics and then finish the set with technical recovery. As with any other tool, knowing when to use it becomes an essential part of the training prescription.

Ankle Strap

Often referred to as a band, the ankle strap is used to "lock" the ankles in place and keep the legs totally stationary. You will see many triathletes using an old inner tube from their bike as their makeshift band or ankle strap, but I dislike this option because it makes it too easy to cheat. With an old rubber inner tube around your ankles, it is too easy to kick—there is a lot of play in rubber, especially aged rubber— but with the ankle strap (with its Velcro® attachments), it is next to impossible to kick, and you are forced to keep your ankles locked in place. This is for a simple reason: We do not want any kicking during pull sets. With the ankle strap, the buoy, and the snorkel, we are all set to focus on tautness and alignment.

Fins

If there were ever a battle for the most favored swim toy in a triathlete's bag, fins would certainly give the pull buoy a run for its money. After long, hard bike and run sessions, putting on a pair of fins in the pool is a wonderful way to help expedite recovery. At our recovery sessions, we always put on fins for kick/swim sets. None of the kicking is fast—it is all done at a relatively easy to moderate intensity—and it significantly helps loosen the legs and get blood flowing to tired muscles with zero impact upon them. This is key.

Although the primary purpose of fins is to help with recovery, they can also help create fluidity in the swim stroke, especially for those swimmers still learning the basics of stroke mechanics and timing. In addition, they can help teach you how to kick properly or how to improve your kick.

One word of warning: There are lots of fins on the market, and not all are appropriate for triathletes. You want to ensure the fins you have are relatively sturdy along the sides, have a medium-length blade, and are pliable. The sturdiness along the sides helps with ankle flexibility, and the length of the blade helps with kick cadence. Avoid fins with short or extremely long (dive style) blades. In my experience, short-bladed fins place heavier stress on the lower back—not optimal. Long-bladed fins slow the kick cadence and encourage a greater angle in the bend of the knee—technically inefficient.

I have no single go-to fin or brand , but many work well for triathletes after they have honed their kicking technique.

Tech Paddles

I have never been a huge advocate for most triathletes swimming with paddles. I do believe they have a place in the swim training of professional triathletes and elite age-groupers but only for those swimming at a certain standard. I consider this standard to be faster than 27 minutes for a 70.3 swim, fewer than 56 minutes for an Ironman swim, and below 20 minutes for a 1,500-meter swim. If you can't swim that fast, then you should not be swimming with paddles. Far too many mid-pack swimmers wear oversized paddles in hopes of becoming faster, but I simply do not believe the bulk of triathletes will get faster by attaching dinner plates to their hands.

Many triathletes who swim above these times have low hand tension and great wrist bending and are improperly levered with their elbows at or below their hands. Adding an oversized paddle does nothing to improve these technical flaws but rather promotes further inefficiency because of the athlete's lack of specific muscular endurance and swim power. For this reason, I see most paddles, specifically those larger than your hands, as highly ineffective. Don't get caught up in following what other athletes do; that doesn't make it correct.

Despite the above, I discovered a technical paddle perfect for swimmers of all abilities. Although it looks a little different than the standard paddle, it helps create a feel for the water unlike any other item of equipment I've encountered so far. You wrap your hand around a spindle while the paddle itself rests against your forearm. You are essentially swimming with a closed hand or fist, and this helps to remove the sensation of your hand catching the water, desensitizing it. Instead, it places the pressure on your wrist and gives a sensation and a feel of engagement of the forearm while swimming. Because of this paddle's design, it prohibits the wrist from bending at ineffective angles. It also helps keep your elbow above your wrist. Its awkward design, specifically the spindles and where the paddle sits, can create a feeling of being off-balance, but in my experience this helps encourage proper tautness and alignment.

We incorporate work with these paddles into shorter distance swims. They might take a bit of getting used to, but after you get accustomed to them, you will immediately feel the benefits—especially when you remove the paddles and resume normal swimming. The feeling is sensational!

Finis Tempo Trainer

This small device has a metronome that emits a beeping sound. It is placed under your swim cap or clipped to your goggle straps and helps govern stroke rate and arm cadence. It has three different mode settings, but we always use it in mode three, which allows you to set the number of strokes per minute (spm). One right-arm stroke counts as one stroke, one left-arm stroke counts as two strokes, and so on.

To learn your stroke rate, set the beep to 60, which is around average, and then without changing your regular swim cadence, listen to establish if your normal rate matches the beep or if it is faster or slower than the beep. If your rate is faster, adjust the beep upward. If slower, then decrease the beep. After a few adjustment trials, you'll soon establish your normal cadence. After you have established this, then it's time to discover how and why we use the Tempo Trainer to help increase or decrease stroke rate (also referred to as arm turnover).

Most triathletes need to increase their stroke rate. After we have established your current stroke rate, we would look to increase it by 5 percent every three weeks without compromising too much efficiency. This will feel hard at first—in fact, it may even seem unattainable—but over time you will adapt. If you are swimming three times a week, you can expect adaptation to take about three weeks. After you get accustomed to the new stroke rate and feel ready to progress, you can work at pushing it up another 5 percent.

There is no specific number to be aiming for; rather, we are looking for an increase in stroke rate until efficiency becomes too compromised and your velocity is reduced. Velocity is a function of stroke rate multiplied by efficiency. We can decrease efficiency after stroke rate makes up for it—and then the question becomes its sustainability. For example, many Level 1 swimmers can hold 90 spm for 25 meters, but for some it might not be sustainable much beyond this distance.

Your stroke rate will increase through training, both from your improved ability to produce more power with each arm stroke (so you are swimming farther with each arm pull), and your increased stroke rate because of your greater power. Therefore, velocity really ramps up as both efficiency and stroke rate shift higher; remember they are multipliers. This then leads to a chicken-and-egg situation—which to work on first, or which to work on more—efficiency, stroke rate, or more power? That's the art, and not the science, and it is often where inexperienced coaches can get tripped up.

We use the Tempo Trainer in many main swim sets during our build, sharpening, and race-ready phases. When the set involves shorter distances, such as 25 or 50 meters, we set the Tempo Trainer higher, that is, at a faster stroke rate, so you learn to generate speed and power over shorter distances with a higher arm turnover. For example, you might swim at 90 spm for a set of fast 25-yard/meter intervals, but your "regular" stroke rate or race-pace stroke rate would be 65 spm. The key to determining your race-pace stroke rate is ascertaining what is sustainable. You might be able to hold 80 spm for four laps, but can you maintain it for 40? Therein lies your answer.

StrechCordz®

As highlighted in Chapter 7, on swim-specific strength and mobility, StrechCordz are a great warm-up tool that helps activate the body for swimming. They also build swim-specific muscular endurance, resilience, and power.

StrechCordz are two hand paddles attached to bungee cords that can be looped around any immoveable object. On dry land, you draw the paddles back until the rope is taut, put your hands into the paddles, bend at the waist with your knees slightly bent, and begin moving your arms as if swimming. Of course, using the correct technique is of utmost importance, and we have a video demonstration available on our Tower 26 YouTube channel. Step-by-step guidelines are also featured in Chapter 7.

The first time you use StrechCordz, I would advise keeping your reps to 30. Ultimately, you'll be aiming to get up to 100 reps at a time for three to five rounds, resting between sets. It will certainly take time to get up to the 100 mark, but with gentle progression over several weeks, it is achievable. If initially 30 reps are too difficult, then there is either too much tension on the cords or the rubber's strength is too great for you.

StrechCordz fire up your shoulders, arms, and lats so that all of your major swimming muscle groups are warmed up and ready to go when it's time to swim. They have the added benefit of being extremely portable and convenient to carry to a race and use as a pre-race warm-up tool. In an age when race warm-ups are often cut short or not offered at all, StrechCordz are a great asset for any triathlete. There is one caveat here: Please ensure you are accustomed to warming up with them before using them at a race. If you've not been using them in training and haven't adapted to them, you could bring on early fatigue before your race has even begun.

Neoprene Swim Shorts

Also known as "cheat shorts" and "floaty shorts," neoprene swim shorts are often a common sight at our Los Angeles pool on recovery swim days. They provide great buoyancy, similar to that of a wet suit. In my experience, they help with recovery on lighter training days, elevating legs in the water that might be heavy and fatigued from high bike and run mileage. They also help athletes get used to the feeling of swimming in a wet suit and the different buoyancy levels and body position that brings. Although they are not part of our swim equipment offering, they are allowed during these recovery sessions but not encouraged or discouraged. We only prohibit them during key A training sessions.

THE TOWER 26 PROGRAM

When I started the Tower 26 program in Los Angeles, I had a vision of how I would ultimately like it to look, and in the past few years that vision has become a reality. In the first year, Tower 26 consisted of me coaching solo on the pool deck with anywhere from 30 to 60 swimmers in attendance. By year two, I brought on my assistant coach, Todd Larlee, to help with more than 100 athletes as triathlon gained popularity.

I knew that if I was going to launch an online program, I wanted to do it the right way, that is, I did not want the program to be like so many of the online offerings triathlon coaches farm out to their athletes. I wanted it to be as close as possible to being here in Los Angeles, and to do this, I knew we needed a lot of high-quality video and audio content so athletes could watch and listen to vital information before beginning their sessions. I also knew I wanted it to be scalable, so that each workout could be executed by triathletes all over the world, regardless of their ability or fitness level, when it was convenient for them.

We wanted to create the *Be Race Ready* podcast so it could serve as a coaching and educational resource athletes could refer to before workouts. It took more than a year of podcasts before we launched the Tower 26 online program in 2017. By this time we had more than 20 hours of swim-specific triathlon content: not only podcasts but also audio files and videos. Each online workout includes an educational audio file, all of which are 6–10 minutes in length, and the videos are all 15 seconds to 3.5 minutes in duration. It has grown to become a huge educational resource, with approximately one hundred teaching videos and a thousand audio files. I also wanted to ensure the online program captured the interactive part of our community, so athletes are encouraged to leave feedback and comments after each swim. This is a great way for a coach to understand how their athletes responded to the workout, and all users have this opportunity—it is up to them how extensively they use it.

At Tower 26 we offer three technical products:

1. A swim lesson involving an assessment of your tautness, alignment, and propulsion (TAP). This subjective information isn't quantifiable but is important nonetheless.
2. A swim consultation of broader scope than a lesson—more of an overall diagnostic, in which we look at your technical ability, training history, frequency of sessions, volume, duration, and training prescription. We do these in person or remotely.
3. Video analysis (either live or online), which includes a full technical diagnostic and 30-day follow-up to see if changes have taken hold.

We now have more than 70 podcasts available for download. If you're keen to dive into these, I would suggest starting with those outlined below, but also searching for additional podcasts relating to TAP and open water:

PODCAST 4 ▸	Technique: Tautness
PODCAST 5 ▸	Technique: Alignment
PODCAST 6 ▸	Technique: Propulsion
PODCAST 9 ▸	Kicking
PODCAST 10 ▸	Breathing Mechanics
PODCASTS 11, 12, 13 ▸	Open-Water Essentials
PODCAST 33 ▸	Open-Water Optimization
PODCAST 52 ▸	Open-Water Skills for the Triathlete

ACKNOWLEDGMENTS

There are three distinct categories for me when it comes to acknowledgments—true professionals, trust, and family.

True professionals and influencers

My former coaches have greatly influenced my career. My own coaching style reflects much of what and how I was taught, and some things I wanted to approach differently: the late Mr. Peter Samuel (Trinidad), coach Geoffrey Ferreira (Trinidad), the late coach Flip Darr (Mission Viejo), coach Mark Schubert (Mission Viejo), and coach Rick Goeden (Los Angeles).

It takes hard work and cooperation for a book to come together: Renee Jardine and her VeloPress team are incredible. Leadership starts at the top; thank you RJ, you are a relentless leader. Emma-Kate Lidbury, book author, former pro triathlete at Tower 26, and friend—this project would have never happened without you. Thank you dearly!

Christophe Balestra, Tower 26 member, retired CEO at Naughty Dog. You created an online platform that reaches athletes around the globe, allowing athletes everywhere to learn from us. I am eternally indebted to you for this.

Trust

Trust is earned, but trusting me with your athletes inspires me further. Thank you: coach Matt Dixon (Purple Patch Fitness), coach Jim Vance, coach Mike Collins (Irvine Novas), and coach Scott DeFilipis (KIS coaching). Our Tower 26 coaching staff, in particular Jim Lubinski, my podcast partner and head triathlon coach. And to the first three triathletes I coached back in the early 1980s: Mike Durkin, Scott Edwards, and Kevin Steele; thank you. Those friendships last a lifetime. Dr. Richard Hoford, a lifelong friend and swim buddy from age 8; your heart beats within me. Gaylene Rey, you taught me in 1984, and then trusted me with your clients. I was a pup then. Thank you dearly.

Family

To my parents, George and Diane Rodrigues, still living in Trinidad, who made the commitment to my training in spite of my dad working 80-hour weeks; thank you for all your dedication. It still guides me today. My brother Brendan and cousin Herman for your unwavering support. And my wife, Elizabeth, who props me up and believes in my dreams; your unequivocal devotion is mind-blowing. And finally, my two kids, Alex and Erin, adults now; hard work has a payoff, it just takes longer for some.

ABOUT THE AUTHORS

GERRY RODRIGUES is the guru of open-water swimming. As head coach of the prestigious Tower 26 swimming and triathlon program based in Santa Monica, California, Rodrigues is the swimming technique expert behind top triathlon coaches such as Matt Dixon (Purple Patch Fitness), Jim Vance, Scott DeFilipis of KIS Coaching, Rad Hallman (head coach, USC Triathlon), celebrity open-water swimmers, and many high-performing professional and age-group triathletes.

Rodrigues grew up swimming off the Caribbean island of Trinidad, where he won many open-water ocean swimming races and earned an athletic scholarship to Pepperdine University. He won the US Masters Swimming National Championship, set several US and world masters swimming records, and has won more than a hundred open-water swimming races.

When he started coaching triathletes in the early 1980s, Rodrigues helped found the first triathlon club in Los Angeles, Team Malibu, and organized the Malibu Masters Swim Club. He cofounded the World Open Water Swimming Association, has managed and coached numerous swimming clubs and teams in Southern California, and has coached dozens of swimmers to top 10 national rankings, national championship wins, national and world records, and Olympic gold medals and world championships.

EMMA-KATE LIDBURY is a journalist, editor, and former professional triathlete. She was coached by Gerry Rodrigues at Tower 26 during the peak of her racing career, which brought her six Ironman 70.3 titles and two top-10 finishes at the Ironman 70.3 World Championships.

Originally from the United Kingdom, Emma-Kate began her journalism career in the British newspaper industry, where she worked for several regional newspapers. She was assigned to cover the Blenheim Triathlon in 2005, and after participating in the race, she was inspired to pause her journalism career to focus her attention on becoming a professional triathlete. She continued to work as a freelance writer in the endurance sports and triathlon space, writing for publications and websites around the world.

She moved to the United States in 2013, landing in Santa Monica, California, where she joined Tower 26 and has since swum nearly 2,000 miles as part of the program. She now lives in Boulder, Colorado, with her husband, Aaron, and their mischievous puppies, Indie and River.

SPECIAL THANKS

KATHLEEN HOHWALD, Tower 26 athlete and former Cornell swim team member. Kathleen's high cadence and overall tactical savvy makes her formidable in any open-water field.

ALEX KOSTICH, friend, decorated Stanford athlete, and former USA national team member. With more overall open-water swim victories than anyone I know, Alex has one of the most powerful open-water swim strokes with incredible stroke/body connection, generating massive torque.

JIM LUBINSKI, former professional ice hockey player, is a pro triathlete and heads up the Tower 26 Triathlon Training Program. He is my trusted coaching and podcast partner, a friend, and is a perfect example of how a rock can actually swim well.

MEGAN MALGAARD, former University of Florida 16-minute-mile swimmer and USA national team member. An outstanding athlete, coach, and business mind, Megan is invaluable and irreplaceable at Tower 26.

BE RACE READY WITH

TOWER 26

Providing swim, bike, run and triathlon coaching to participants in Los Angeles and online enthusiasts of all levels across the world.

TOWER26.COM

VISIT
VELOPRESS.COM

for more on running, cycling, triathlon,
swimming, ultrarunning,
yoga, recovery, mental training,
health and fitness, nutrition, and diet.

SAVE $10
ON YOUR FIRST ORDER

Shop with us and use coupon code
VPFIRST during checkout.